CHIASMA

A Site For Thought

#5

TO BE A BODY?

Chiasma: A Site For Thought Vol. 5, Issue 5: To Be a Body?
ISBN: 978-0-7714-3126-5 (Print)
ISBN: 978-0-7714-3127-2 (Online)
ISSN: 2292-6887 (Print)
ISSN: 2292-6925 (Online)

Layout and Cover Design by M. Curtis Allen

CHIASMA

Chiasma: A Site For Thought is housed in Western University's Centre for the Study of Theory and Criticism

TABLE OF CONTENTS

Editor's Introduction 8
M. Curtis Allen

CONTRIBUTIONS

Bodies That Matter?: From Embodied Subjectivity to Materialism in Merleau-Ponty's Political Philosophy 14
Anne Van Leeuwen

Distinction, Participation, and Empty Embodiment 43
Adam Lovasz

Embodied Experience of Multiplicitous Selfhood 59
Mariana Ortega interviewed by Julian Evans, Jessica Ellis, and Sangie Zaitsoff

The Relationship of Temporality in Autobiography to Trans-Narrative Form 73
Jessica Ellis

Gender Identity Trouble: An Analysis of the Under-Representation of Trans* Professors in Canadian Universities 90
Alexandre Baril translated by Hélène Bigras Dutrisac and David Guignion

Ways of Being in the All-Too-Present Body 129
A. Rebecca Rozelle-Stone

Objects That Matter: Bodies, Art, and Big Data 155
Katherine Behar interviewed by Anna Mirzayan

REVIEWS

Brian Kim Stefans, *Word Toys* 171
John Nyman

Mariana Ortega, *In-Between: Latina Feminist Phenomenology, Multiplicity, and the Self* 178
Helen Fielding

Cindy Zeiher and Todd McGowan, *Can Philosophy Love?* 190
Ali Alizadeh

EDITOR'S INTRODUCTION

For the quinary issue of *Chiasma*, we ask what it means "To Be a Body?". The theme of embodiment in theoretical and speculative thought is as broad as the subjects it comes into contact with. Yet, in almost all domains of experience and understanding, the conceptualization of embodiment and the body have been radically transformed by the past four hundred years—transformations that have continued to intensify in the last few decades. Embodiment, therefore, has become an unyielding issue to think adequately in the 21st century, and one on which there is as yet little agreement; not only as to what it means to be a body, but also on what is at stake in being one. The advance of technological dispersion and prosthesis, the speculative proposals of a world without bodies (or of technological singularity), a historical moment of unprecedented aging populations in the West, the discourses of health, biopolitical apparatuses and governance, the movement and diaspora of peoples throughout the world, as well as the increasingly diffuse regulation of bodies and their movement all pose dilemmas to the thought of the body.

On the other hand, embodiment poses equally profound questions about the status of the mind, of thought, and of the 'nature' or ground of epistemological, intentional, and agentic claims. To what extent is the particularity of our thought the artifact of our bodies? And to what extent can we exercise freedom over our corporeal determinations? How does the artificialization of cognitive processes trouble traditional ideas about the inextricability of mind and embodiment? How do the policing and control of feminized and non-conforming bodies determine and articulate sexism and gender inequalities? What do queer theory and the study of trans identity teach us about embodiment? What relation should we have to the many historical "despisers of the body"[1] who nevertheless rank among the greatest thinkers in Western philosophy? To what extent should the field of phenomenology be taken up from the precept of embodiment? Is embodiment a real site of immediacy in lived experience or is embodiment itself mediated, abstracted, or alienated? To what extent are bodies and embodiment themselves theoretical constructs? Finally, how do we envision embodiment in the broader context of its environment (proprioceptive, cultural, social, political, ecological)? Any one of these questions could, no doubt, fill its own volume, but the gravity and scope of the issues here only impels us toward a general appeal in coming to terms with the problematic of embodiment. The ubiquity with which contemporary thought about the body touches on our social totality and intercedes into the fabric of our lives makes imperative the need to take stock of its theoretical breadth synoptically. Here we attempt only to begin such a venture.

Thus, in the pages that follow, many varying approaches to embodiment and its implications are thoroughly examined. Anne Van Leeuwen's "Bodies That Matter?" ushers us into the issue with a discussion of the imbrication of embodiment, materialism, and Marxist politics in the work of Merleau-Ponty. There she argues against the tide of both historical necessity and voluntarist politics by reasserting the emergence of embodied subjectivity in the social interplay between historical conditions, forces of production, and acts of collective agency which make up the materialist dialectic of the proletariat, properly understood, as that of "the constitutive

1 Friedrich Nietzsche, "On the Despisers of the Body, "*Thus Spoke Zarathustra* in *The Portable Nietzsche,* Trans. Walter Kaufmann, New York: Penguin (1976), 146-8.

ambiguity… which cannot be resolved." Thus, for Van Leeuwen, embodiment as class struggle—much like the 'permanent revolution'—is that which produces its history by virtue of its own persistent interrogation.

Following in its course, we have Adam Lovasz's "Distinction, Participation, and Empty Embodiment." The article is a meditation on two apparently antithetical understandings of the body: as subjectified (or self-having) on the one hand, and the purely material (or inert and without self) on the other. Between these, ancient Buddhist philosopher Nagarjuna's *madhyamika* (middle way) provides a nonconceptual synthesis of these mutually exclusive conceptual understandings. Further, Lovasz employs the attendant notion of emptiness, alongside recent work on psychosexual behaviour, in ethology, and enactive cognition to experimentally rewrite an experiential, ethical, overcoming of this theoretical matrix of the body.

Third in the issue is an interview—conducted by Julian Evans, Jessica Ellis, and Sangie Zaitsoff—with Latina feminist phenomenologist Mariana Ortega entitled, "Embodied Experience of Multiplicitous Selfhoood." There she discusses her conception of 'multiplicitous selfhood' as it is tied to the lived experience of the Latina woman. Importantly, her concept allows an incisive critique of the three disciplines which have come to shape Ortega's thought as an embodied thinker in the world: phenomenology, feminism, and Latinx studies. These latter two deploy important correctives—imbued with sensitivity to the singularity of lived encounter, and all the political weight that it comes with—to the neutral, transcendental, bodiless, subject of traditional phenomenology. Latinx experience, on the other hand, provides a useful critique and refinement of the work being done by intersectional feminists, in which the sections (race, class, gender, etc.) typically brought together in the intersectional approach are still thought as mutually extricable; the concept of multiplicity offers Ortega a way out of this implicitly divisive tactic without losing sight of the target it aims at, and the real and profound effects on the lived experiences of marked bodies that such precarious selves feel. Ortega offers thoughts on her continued debt to Heidegger, fraught though it is, as well as on how her theoretical work makes contact with the politics of immigration and the escalating racism of Trump's America.

Next is Jessica Ellis' "The Relation of Temporality in Autobiography to Trans-Narrative Form." Ellis converges on recent Trans and queer theory as well as on a Bakhtin-inspired approach to narratology to delve into the embodiment of temporality as it is put to discourse. Using Bakhtin's 'chronotope' to analyze historical temporality in trans-narrative becomes itself a clarion call to revolutionary politics, and a theoretical point of departure in the analysis of historical-political paradigm shifts. Through it, Ellis aims for "a change in the diagnostic language from gender dysphoria to gender dissonance... In this way gender is not seen as an individual's internal—and pathological—struggle, but rather part of the greater social context from which gender is reinforced and how this oppresses non-cisgender folk."

Following Ellis, we have a translation—by Hélène Bigras-Dutrisac and David Guignon—of Quebec sociologist Alexandre Baril's "Gender Identity Trouble: An Analysis of the Underrepresentation of Trans* Professors in Canadian Universities." Baril examines many of the parameters and case studies which concretely make evident the lack of trans* persons in Canadian academia, even in the case of tenured experts in the fields which comprise Trans* studies. Here Baril goes to great lengths, with extreme rigour, to problematize the very field of cultural production which should, by definition, be least susceptible to these systemic and structural biases. Baril's article is an invitation to assess the value of the organizational structures of our institutions and their hiring practices, as much as it is a brutal reminder of the unequal distribution of the precarity of embodiment in its social coding.

"Ways of Being in the All-Too-Present Body" gives us an elaboration of the phenomenology of chronic pain, and its philosophical dimensions. In it, A. Rebecca Rozelle-Stone engages the work of Susan Wendell and Simone Weil, among others, in evoking the absurdity of life through pain, all the while affirming that same suffering as an "accidental and material education" with profoundly moral, epistemic, metaphysical, and, indeed, spiritual consequences.

Lastly, our Contributions section is bookended by a title the inverse of that which inaugurated it. Anna Mirzayan interviews multimedia artist and thinker Katherine Behar in "Objects that Matter: Bodies, Art, and Big Data" where Behar details her thoughts on the relationship between embodiment and the contemporary technologies which affect it, her own contributions to the field of Object Oriented Feminism, the issue of speed in politics, as well as the ways in which the conceptual and algorithmic framing of big data identity markers in some sense mirrors the uses of intersectionality in recent feminist discourse. With the proliferation of ever more technological mediations of experience and embodiment, Behar's indicative analyses here point toward the need for us to continue to think both widely and deeply about the meaning, value, and nature of corporeality as it is spread across the social body today.

Our Reviews section features a critical engagement with Brian Kim Stefans' *Word Toys* where John Nyman relates the book to the history of avant-garde poetics and the technics of the text. The issue also includes Helen Fielding's review of Ortega's *In Between: Latina Feminist Phenomenology, Multiciplicity, and the Self*, in which Fielding outlines and elaborates many of the conceptual themes discussed and applied in the interview. Lastly, Ali Alizadeh reviews an anthology—edited by Cindy Zeiher and Todd McGowan—on the relationship between philosophy and love, aptly titled, *Can Philosophy Love?* which discusses the major Continental thinkers on love of the past three centuries: Rousseau, Hegel, Lacan, Badiou, and others all find their place in the panoply of the love of wisdom of love.

All the editors of *Chiasma* would like to offer their deep gratitude to the Centre for the Study of Theory and Criticism at Western University for its continued funding and support, and in particular to Dr. Allan Pero, whose aid, advice, and impeccable command of the English language is always sincerely appreciated.

We would also like to thank Melanie Caldwell for her unerring professionalism. Our advisory board continues to encourage our venture, while providing excellent and insightful commentary, for which we truly thank them. We must also thank our many anonymous peer reviewers who ensured that our fifth issue maintains the high standards the journal sets for itself. Finally, and most of all, we would like to thank all our contributors, without whom *Chiasma* would scarcely be possible.

Thank you.

– M. Curtis Allen, Chief Editor

BODIES THAT MATTER?

From Embodied Subjectivity to Materialism in Merleau-Ponty's Political Philosophy

ANNE VAN LEEUWEN

1. From Existential-Phenomenology to Politics

Maurice Merleau-Ponty is often regarded as the preeminent thinker of embodiment in the tradition of twentieth century phenomenology. In his chef-d'œuvre, *Phenomenology of Perception* (*Phénoménologie de la perception*, 1945), he defends existential-phenomenology as a theory of the subject, while distinguishing the existential-phenomenological subject from idealist and empiricist philosophies of consciousness—positions that he refers to as "idealist reflection" and "objective thought," respectively. For both transcendental idealism and empirical psychology, the subject is abstract—referring either to the ideality of a transcendental subject or an equally abstract materiality.[1] Merleau-Ponty argues that the existential-phenomenological subject refers neither to transcendental consciousness that is revealed by analytical reflection nor to the functions of the brain that are disclosed by empirical psychology and neuroscience. Phenomenology, he claims, offers a "third way" out of the impasse of this debate between idealist reflection and objective thought,[2]

1 The subject understood as the cognitive functions of the brain.

2 This is Lukács's interpretation (and critique) of existential-phenomenology—i.e., that it merely attempts to be a "third way" beyond idealism and materialism. See Lukács, "Existentialism," in *Marxism and Human Liberation* (New York: Delta, 1973), 244. While Lukács is critical of existential-phenomenology for this reason, I will try to argue that Merleau-Ponty's "third way" leads him directly to Lukács's understanding of the materialist dialectic. I

and the subject disclosed by phenomenological inquiry subverts the metaphysical binaries that plague these debates. As such, he argues that the phenomenological subject must be conceived of as constitutively embodied, situated and historical.

While Merleau-Ponty's analysis of the embodied subject has been the focus of intensive scholarship, the political stakes of his theory of the subject have been less extensively explored.[3] The final chapter of *Phenomenology of Perception*, however, brings into view the fundamental connection between the constitutively situated and embodied subject of his phenomenological analyses and his nascent materialist politics. In the final chapter on freedom, Merleau-Ponty elucidates his theory of the subject in the context of an analysis of class-consciousness. Here he describes the existential-phenomenological subject as not only embodied and situated but also irreducibly historical, i.e., as inextricably bound to its historical conditions. Freedom, he argues, is not freedom from history but within it. In capitalist modernity, this means that the subject is bound to the historical conditions of commodity production and its constitutive class structure, granting the subject the possibility of grasping the significance of its position vis-à-vis this structure at the level of action. On the basis of this analysis, the phenomenological subject emerges in the final chapter of *Phenomenology of Perception* as the subject of materialist politics.

Merleau-Ponty continues to develop this theory of the subject in his political writings from 1945-1955. In the essay "Marxism and Philosophy" ("Marxisme et philosophie," 1945-1947), he identifies a parallel between his own critique of both idealism and objective thought and Marx's repudiation of both idealism and vulgar materialism. Drawing on Lukács's reading of Marx in *History and Class Consciousness* (*Geschichte und Klassenbewußtsein*, 1923)

come back to this point on, see footnote 20.

3 There have of course been significant debates around the import of Merleau-Ponty's analysis of embodied subjectivity for feminist theory. See, for example, Silvia Stoller, "Reflections on Feminist Merleau-Ponty Skepticism," *Hypatia* 15, no.1 (2000), 175-182. What this article examines, however, is the relationship between Merleau-Ponty's analysis of embodied subjectivity and his commitments to a materialist politics.

and his analysis of the materialist dialectic, Merleau-Ponty seizes upon the dialectic as a way to obviate the binary oppositions of metaphysics: consciousness/matter, thought/action, knowledge/history. In this essay, it becomes clear that the materialist dialectic is essential for Merleau-Ponty to fully realize the project of *Phenomenology of Perception*, i.e., to theorize the phenomenological subject beyond the subjectivism of idealist reflection and the vulgar materialism of objective thought.

Humanism and Terror (*Humanisme et terreur*, 1947) and *Adventures of the Dialectic* (*Les Aventures de la dialectique*, 1955) develop these earlier insights in different directions. Yet by tracing the evolution of Merleau-Ponty's thought and his analysis of the materialist dialectic from *Phenomenology of Perception* to *Adventures of the Dialectic,* I will identify the embodied subject of *Phenomenology of Perception* as the basis of his later analysis of the peculiar ontological status of the commodity form, i.e., what he identifies in his political writing as the self-consciousness of the commodity (*l'autoconnaissance de la merchandise*). For Merleau-Ponty, the materialist dialectic ultimately points to the self-consciousness *of* history that cannot be resolved into either subject or object according to the parameters of idealist reflection or objective thought. In this way, it offers a philosophy of history as permanent self-interrogation. What he describes in *Adventures of the Dialectic* as the "ambiguity of the dialectic"[4] represents the realization of the embodied subject of phenomenology that we find in *Phenomenology of Perception.* This interpretation thus departs from standard readings of Merleau-Ponty in two ways: first, it suggests that Merleau-Ponty's ontological commitments cannot be bifurcated from his political commitments—and more precisely, that his earlier philosophy of embodied subjectivity is indissociable from his materialist philosophy of history in his later thought; second, it claims that Merleau-Ponty's self-avowed renewed faith in liberalism in his later work is belied by his persistent commitment to a materialist dialectic.[5]

4 Ibid., 69.

5 This interpretation differs most sharply from standard readings of Merleau-Ponty's political philosophy largely because it attempts to rethink

2. Freedom and Class-Consciousness

In the final chapter of *Phenomenology of Perception*, Merleau-Ponty's discussion of freedom once again attempts to circumvent the dichotomy between objective thought and idealist reflection. In the context of the issue of freedom, these two poles manifest, respectively, as the commitment to a material, scientific account of causality, on one hand, and "the assertion of an absolute freedom divorced from the outside,"[6] on the other. For objective thought, the existence of freedom is impossible, while for idealist reflection freedom is boundless and unconditioned. Contra these two extremes, Merleau-Ponty seeks to make sense of what he identifies as the constitutively situated nature of freedom—that "there is no freedom without a field."[7] What this means, according to Merleau-Ponty, is that freedom refers neither to the abstract and unconditioned freedom of pure consciousness nor is it annulled by material-causal determinism. As he puts it:

> The world is already constituted, but also never completely constituted; in the first case we are acted upon, in the second we are open to an infinite number of possibilities. But this analysis is still abstract, for we exist in both ways at once. There is, therefore, never determinism and never absolute choice. I am never a thing and never a bare consciousness.[8]

---

what, for Merleau-Ponty, is the philosophical core of Marxism. Unlike other readers of Merleau-Ponty, I argue that the key to understanding his interpretation of the materialist dialectic is Marx's analysis of the commodity form in *Capital* and its interpretation in the work of Lukács. Ultimately, my interpretation of dialectic in Merleau-Ponty's thought comes closest to Barry Cooper's reading in *Merleau-Ponty and Marxism: From Terror to Reform.* (Toronto: University of Toronto Press, 1979). As Cooper puts it, citing Merleau-Ponty: "A thematised and predicated dialectic is a 'bad' dialectic, and 'and this is what happens when the *meaning and sense* (*sens*) of dialectical movement is defined apart from the concrete constellation."

6 Maurice Merleau-Ponty, *Phenomenology of Perception* (New York; London: Routlege, 2002), 507.

7 Ibid., 510.

8 Ibid., 527. See Keith Whitmoyer's *The Philosophy of Ontological Lateness: Merleau-Ponty and the Tasks of Thinking* (Bloomsbury, 2017), for the most systematic and developed elaboration of this aspect of Merleau-Ponty's thought

Merleau-Ponty's claim is that the very shape and form that freedom takes is dependent on its being situated in the world, i.e., freedom is literally formless without the bond that embeds it within the world. As he puts it in the essay "Marxism and Philosophy": "it is a matter of understanding that the bond which attaches man to the world is at the same time his way to freedom."[9]

Merleau-Ponty attempts to elaborate his account of freedom in *Phenomenology of Perception* vis-à-vis the phenomenon of class-consciousness. In this discussion, he rejects both a positivist view of history that he identifies with objective thought along with the abstract view offered by idealist reflection. From the standpoint of objective thought, class-consciousness is reducible to the conditions of production; as such, the positions of the proletariat and the bourgeoisie are identical with their objective positions within the system of production. Class-consciousness becomes an epiphenomenon of these conditions and the revolutionary action of the proletariat merely an index of the inexorable unfolding of the logic of history. In contrast, according idealist reflection, class-consciousness is reducible to a choice or decision on the part of the abstract subject of consciousness—e.g., one is a proletarian or bourgeois to the extent that he or she chooses to view his or her position vis-à-vis that particular optic. On the latter view, revolutionary action is supplanted by the *idea* of class-consciousness insofar as to be proletarian it suffices to understand the phenomenon of exploitation and to take up this view of history in an act of judgment.[10]

In contrast with these two views, Merleau-Ponty argues for what he describes as an "existential" understanding of class-con-

in *Phenomenology of Perception*.

9 Maurice Merleau-Ponty, "Marxism and Philosophy," in *Sense and Non-Sense*, trans. Hubert Dreyfus and Patricia Allen Dreyfus (Evanston: Northwestern University Press, 1964), 130.

10 As Merleau-Ponty puts it, "[t]o make class-consciousness the outcome of a decision and a choice is to say that problems are solved on the day they are posed, that every question already contains the reply that it awaits; it is, in short, to revert to immanence and abandon the attempt to understand history." Merleau-Ponty, *Phenomenology of Perception*, 519.

sciousness. According to him,

> I am not conscious of being working class or middle class simply because, as a matter of fact, I sell my labor or, equally as a matter of fact, because my interests are bound up with capitalism, nor do I become one or the other on the day on which I elect to view history in light of the class struggle: what happens is that 'I exist as working class' or 'I exist as middle class' in the first place, and it is this mode of dealing with the world and society which provides both the motives for my revolutionary or conservative projects and my explicit judgments of the type: 'I am working class' or 'I am middle class', without it being possible to deduce the former from the latter, or vice versa. What makes me a proletarian is not the economic system or the society considered as systems of impersonal forces, but these institutions as I carry them within me and experience them; nor is it an intellectual operation devoid of motive, but my way of being in the world within this institutional framework.[11]

His point is that class-consciousness cannot be reduced to the expression of objective conditions—"it is never the case that my objective position in the production process is sufficient to awaken class-consciousness"[12]—but neither is it simply the result of an intellectual project or voluntarist decision to view history through a Marxist lens. Rather, class-consciousness refers to the experience of exploitation within the system of production that is fundamental to existence within capitalism. Insofar as existence within capitalism is fundamentally structured by my class position, this experience of being proletarian or being bourgeois constitutes the motivational horizon of all of my existential projects without necessarily being made thematic.[13] What this means is that I exist as proletarian or bourgeois, i.e., being proletarian or bourgeois is

11 Ibid., 515.

12 Ibid., 514.

13 This is why, he argues, that revolutionary action should not be conceived of as an intellectual project but rather an existential one, consisting in "the polarization of life towards a goal which is both determinate and indeterminate, which, to the person concerned, is entirely unrepresented, and which is recognized only on being attained" (Ibid., 518).

endemic to my mode of being in the world and my relations with others, and it is this experience that is prior to, and the ground of, any thetic judgment I might make about capitalism.

Here we return to Merleau-Ponty's broader claim that freedom exists only within a field. Consciousness is not simply derived from class relations, as vulgar materialism would suggest, and thus freedom is not simply chimerical. Neither is it the case, however, that I first exist as consciousness in the abstract—free and unconditioned—and only secondarily exist within the historical conditions of the system of production, i.e., as proletarian or bourgeois.[14] As Merleau-Ponty argues,

> At the outset, I am not an individual beyond class, I am situated in a social environment, and my freedom, though it may have the power to commit me elsewhere, has not the power to transform me instantaneously into what I decide to be. Thus to be a bourgeois or a worker is not only to be aware of being one or the other, it is to identify oneself as worker or bourgeois through an implicit existential project which merges into our way of patterning the world and co-existing with other people. My decision draws together a spontaneous meaning of my life which it may confirm or repudiate, but not annul.[15]

The subject of freedom, then, is not the abstract subject of transcendental consciousness—the unconditioned origin and constitutive centre of meaning and significance.[16] Rather, the subject of freedom exists within a socio-historical environment that is structured by a significance that the subject does not constitute, a significance that includes, among other things, the historical conditions of the system of production.[17] To exist within modernity is to exist

14 "Both idealism and objective thinking fail to pin down the coming into being of class-consciousness, the former because it deduces actual existence from consciousness, the latter because it derives consciousness from *de facto* existence, and both because they overlook the relation of motivation" (Ibid., 520).

15 Ibid.

16 "I am all that I see, I am an intersubjective field, not despite my body and historical situation, but, on the contrary, by being this body and this situation, and through them, all the rest." Ibid., 525.

17 "My life must have a significance which I do not constitute; there must

within global capitalism, and thus for the subject of modernity, being proletarian or being bourgeois is not a secondary or derivative mode of existence but fundamental to the existence of this historical subject. Indeed, as Merleau-Ponty points out, "[t]here is therefore no occasion to ask ourselves why the thinking subject or consciousness perceives itself as a man, or an incarnate or historical subject, nor must we treat this apperception as a second order operation which it somehow performs starting from its absolute existence."[18] The experience of class is rather inscribed in the structure and motivation of all of one's existential projects and relations with others—it constitutes what Merleau-Ponty describes as the "spontaneous meaning of my life", i.e., a "significance that I do not constitute."[19] Freedom, he argues, is neither obviated by this spontaneous significance nor does it exist in isolation from it; rather, freedom draws upon this significance. What this means, he argues, is that I am free to confirm my class position by acting in solidarity with others, or to repudiate it by refusing to take up a revolutionary existential project, but I am not free to annul the significance of the socio-historical reality of the conditions that constitute the field of my freedom.

3. Marx's Philosophy and the Dialectic

Merleau-Ponty's essay "Marxism and Philosophy", which was written between 1945 and 1947, functions both chronologically and thematically as a bridge between *Phenomenology of Perception* and *Humanism and Terror*. In this essay Merleau-Ponty returns to the issue of class-consciousness, criticizing what he sees as the tendency of his contemporaries to interpret Marx's philosophy in positivist

strictly speaking be an intersubjectivity; each one of us must be both anonymous in the sense of absolutely individual, and anonymous in the sense of absolutely general. Our being in the world is the concrete bearer of this double anonymity" (Ibid., 521).

18 Ibid., 524.

19 Ibid., 521. That is, as he puts it later, "[t]he *Sinngebung* is not merely centrifugal, which is why the subject of history is not the individual." Ibid., 522.

terms—i.e., "to reduce man to the state of a scientific object."[20] In contrast with this tendency, he insists that Marxism is inimical not only with idealist reflection but also with objective thought, i.e., that Marx's critique of idealism is equally a repudiation of vulgar materialism.[21] In this essay, he appeals to Marx as an ally in his continued critique of both objective thought and idealist reflection.[22] What "Marxism and Philosophy" introduces, however, is a discussion of the materialist dialectic. According to Merleau-Ponty, it is vis-à-vis the materialist dialectic that Marx's philosophy breaks with the tradition of metaphysics and its founding dissociation of "matter" and "consciousness," a dissociation that subtends the positions of both objective thought and idealist reflection. The central import of Marx's dialectic, for Merleau-Ponty, is that matter and consciousness cannot be considered separately.[23] In his turn to the dialectic, Merleau-Ponty's existential-phenomenology ceases to be merely another philosophical attempt to find a "third way" beyond idealism and materialism.[24]

20 Merleau-Ponty, "Marxism and Philosophy," 125.

21 We find this critique of vulgar materialism and "bourgeois voluntarism" or idealist reflection also in Lukács' work: "as the so-called Machists among Marx's supporters have demonstrated, it even reinforces the view that reality with its 'obedience to laws,' in the sense used by bourgeois, contemplative materialism and the classical economics with which it is so closely bound up, is impenetrable, fatalistic and immutable. That Machism can also give birth to an equally bourgeois voluntarism does not contradict this. Fatalism and voluntarism are only mutually contradictory to an undialectical and unhistorical mind" Georg Lukács, *History and Class Consciousness* (Cambridge: MIT Press, 1971), 4.

22 Yet as Merleau-Ponty points out, it is precisely Marx's rejection of vulgar materialism that tends to be missed by contemporary interpreters. What lends credibility to this reading, he suggests, "is that Marx is fighting on two fronts. On the one hand, he is opposed to all forms of mechanistic thought; on the other, he is waging war with idealism." Merleau-Ponty, "Marxism and Philosophy," 128.

23 "The question has sometimes been raised, and with reason, as to how a materialism could be dialectical; how matter, taken in the strict sense of the word, could contain the principle of productivity and novelty which is called dialectic. It is because in Marxism 'matter'—and indeed, 'consciousness'—is never considered separately" Ibid., 129.

24 This is Lukács's interpretation of existential-phenomenology: "mod-

Merleau-Ponty's interpretation of Marx both in this essay and throughout his later work is deeply influenced by Lukács' reading of Marx in *History and Class Consciousness.*[25] Here, Lukács' critique of reification plays a crucial role. Reification, for Lukács, refers to the reduction of all aspects of existence to the form of the commodity—i.e., things, people and their relation to the world and to each other. As such, the phenomenon of reification is specific to the development of capitalism in which the commodity becomes the universal category of social life.[26] Lukács points out that what Marx claims is peculiar to the commodity is its "phantom-like objectivity" or "sensuous super-sensuous" form—i.e., that what is in fact a social relation (the production and exchange of commodities) appears in the form of a thing (the commodity as a congealed quantum of labor-power).[27] In virtue of this form of appearance,

ern phenomenology is one the numerous philosophical methods which seek to rise above both idealism and materialism by discovering a philosophical 'third way,' by making intuition the true source of knowledge" Georg Lukács, "Existentialism," *Marxism and Human Liberation* (New York: Delta, 1973), 244.

25 Not only does Merleau-Ponty cite Lukács's essay "Reification and the Consciousness of the Proletariat", he also uses the same epigraph that Lukács uses in this essay as the epigraph to "Marxism and Philosophy" in *History and Class Consciousness*. Merleau-Ponty's sympathy for Lukács prior to *Adventures of the Dialectic* likely reflects the fact that Lukács's polemic against existentialism and his public feud with Sartre occurs only in 1949 with the publication of "Marxismus und Existentialismus" along with a lecture tour in Paris and a series of interviews conducted in the same year in which Lukács publically denounces Sartre. See for example Mitchell Cohen, "Existentialism, Marxism, Structuralism," in *The Wager of Lucien Goldman* (Princeton: Princeton University Press, 1994), 213. Merleau-Ponty's treatment of Lukács in *Adventures of the Dialectic* is more ambivalent than in his earlier writings.

26 "Only in this context does the reification produced by commodity relations assume decisive importance both for the objective evolution of society and for the stance adopted by men towards it. Only then does the commodity become crucial for the subjugation of men's consciousness to the forms in which this reification finds expression and for their attempts to comprehend the process or to rebel against its disastrous effects and liberate themselves from servitude to the 'second nature' so created" Lukács, *History and Class Consciousness*, 86.

27 According to Marx, "the mysterious character of the commodity-form consists therefore simply in the fact the commodity reflects the social characteristics of men's own labor as objective characteristics of the products

what is in fact a contingent and historically specific form of social relation accrues the appearance of objectivity.[28] This form of appearance is what Marx famously calls "fetishism" and Lukács famously describes as "second nature"—i.e., that because this social relation appears in the form of a thing and thus as objective and immediately given, in the commodity form we seem to confront an autonomous reality that is natural, intransient and immutable. As Lukács puts it:

> [M]an in capitalist society confronts a reality 'made' by himself (as a class) which appears to him to be a natural phenomenon alien to himself; he is wholly at the mercy of its 'laws', his activity is confined to the exploitation of the inexorable fulfillment of certain individual laws for his own (egoistic) interests. But even while 'acting' he remains, in the nature of the case, the object and not the subject of events. The field of his action becomes wholly internalized: it consists on the one hand of the awareness of the laws which he uses and, on the other, of his awareness of his inner reactions to the course taken by events.[29]

The form that the world, the subject and all human relations accrue under the historically specific conditions of generalized commodity of production thereby acquires the objective appearance of a natural phenomenon, i.e., something intractable, unconditioned, and immediately given.[30]

---

of labor themselves, as the socio-natural properties of these things (Karl Marx, *Capital Volume 1: A Critique of Political Economy* [London: Penguin, 1990], 165). By donning the form of useful things, these socio-historical relations of appear as something natural or non-symbolic, what Lukács famously described in *History and Class Consciousness* as "second nature" Lukács, *History and Class Consciousness*, 86.

28 Merleau-Ponty picks up this account of reification in "Marxism and Philosophy". As he puts it, "[t]he bourgeois ideologies which contaminate all of bourgeois society, including its proletariat, are not *appearances*; they mystify bourgeois society and present themselves to it in the guise of a stable world. They are exactly as 'real' as structures of capitalist economy, with which they form a single system" Merleau-Ponty, "Marxism and Philosophy," 132.

29 Ibid., 135.

30 As Merleau-Ponty argues, this same critique of reification applies reflexively to vulgar materialism: "A Marxist political economy can speak of

For Lukács, the universality of the commodity form within capitalist modernity calls for a philosophical method that is adequate to this form—i.e., it impels a shift from metaphysics to dialectic. The founding belief in the immediate givenness of reality as a thing-in-itself is the hallmark of what Lukács calls "bourgeois metaphysics." From the standpoint of metaphysics, subject and object are rigidly opposed, and thought accorded the status of a merely subjective mediation of reality that is unconditioned and immediately given.[31] In contrast, from the standpoint of dialectical thought, objectivity is constituted rather than immediately given, and the mediation of thought is constitutive of the objectivity of the thing. This means, in turn, that mediation is not something merely subjective, "foisted on to the objects from outside,"[32] i.e., it does not refer to subjective judgments of "value" as opposed to how things are in themselves.[33] Rather the object is constitutively mediated: The "empirical existence of objects is itself mediated and only appears to be unmediated in so far as the awareness of mediation is lacking so that the objects are torn from the complex of their true determinants and placed in artificial isolation."[34] A dialectical method thus does not introduce a subjective veil over reality; rather it makes visible a structure of reality that is oth-

laws only within qualitatively distinct structures, which must be described in terms of history. *A priori*, scientism seems a conservative idea since it causes us to mistake the merely momentary for the eternal. Throughout the history of Marxism, in fact, the fetishism of science has always made its appearance where the revolutionary conscience was faltering…As Lukács notes, scientism is a particular case of alienation or objectification (*Verdinglichung*) which deprives man of his human reality and makes him confuse himself with things." Ibid., 126.

31 "The belief that the transformation of the immediately given into a truly understood (and not merely an immediately perceived) and for that reason really objective reality, i.e., the belief that the impact of the category of mediation upon the picture of the world is merely 'subjective', i.e., is no more than an evaluation of a reality that 'remains unchanged', all this is as much to say that objective reality has the character of a thing-in-itself." Lukács, *History and Class Consciousness*, 150.

32 Ibid., 162.

33 Ibid.

34 Ibid., 163.

erwise occluded—i.e., it constitutes "*the manifestation of its objective structure.*"[35] Reality conceived by metaphysical thought as a composite of isolated things immediately given is thereby supplanted by an understanding of the relations that mediate reality and constitute it as a social totality.

Lukács elaborates the phenomenon of class-consciousness in these terms. Class-consciousness does not refer to a merely subjective judgment of the proletariat; rather it is the objective manifestation of the structural conditions that are otherwise elided by the conditions of commodity production. As such, class-consciousness involves the self-knowledge of the worker within this system of production, which is to say, the self-knowledge of the commodity form: "Above all the worker can only become conscious of his existence in society when he becomes aware of himself as a commodity… Inasmuch as he is incapable in practice of raising himself above the role of object his consciousness is the *self-consciousness of the commodity*."[36] Consciousness, then, does not refer to something merely ideational or subjective; rather it refers to the self-understanding of the commodity form.[37] It is this understanding, moreover, that brings about a practical transformation in relations of production. Insofar as self-consciousness is no longer conceived of as knowledge of the object that stands over and against consciousness but as the self-consciousness *of* the object (*das Selbstbewusstsein des Gegenstandes*), consciousness itself involves a practical transformation of that object.[38] As Lukács puts it, "since consciousness here is not the knowledge of an opposed object but is the self-consciousness of the object *the act of consciousness overthrows*

35 Ibid., 162.

36 Ibid., 168.

37 "The specific nature of this kind of commodity had consisted in the fact that beneath the cloak of the thing lay a relation between men, that beneath the quantifying crust there was a qualitative, living core. Now that this core is revealed, it becomes possible to recognize the fetish character of *every commodity* based on the commodity character of labor power." Ibid., 169.

38 This knowledge, he argues, "*brings about an objective structural change in the object of knowledge.*" Ibid.

the objective form of its object."[39]

According to Lukács, then, it is precisely the dialectical method that allows us to understand that class-consciousness is at once constituted by history and at the same time not simply determined by history. As he puts it:

> Since consciousness appears as the immanent product of the historical dialectic, it likewise appears to be dialectical. That is to say, this consciousness is nothing but the expression of historical necessity. The proletariat 'has no ideals to realize'. When its consciousness is put into practice it can only breathe life into the things which the dialectics of history have forced to a crisis; it can never 'in practice' ignore the course of history, forcing on it what are no more than its own desires or knowledge. For it is itself nothing but the contradictions of history that have become conscious. On the other hand, however, a dialectical necessity is far from being the same thing as mechanical, causal necessity... In addition to the mere contradiction—the automatic product of capitalism—a *new* element is required: the consciousness of the proletariat must become deed.[40]

What Lukács argues, then, is that a dialectical view of class-consciousness refuses both the determinism of vulgar Marxism as well as subjectivism of idealist reflection. Rather than something ideational and subjective, class-consciousness refers to the self-understanding *of* history. This does not mean, however, that class-conscious is simply causally determined by its historical situation. Class-conscious involves a transformation in the object of knowledge and thus a transformation of this situation. This transformation takes places vis-à-vis the consciousness of the proletariat in the form of praxis.[41]

---

39 Ibid., 178.

40 Ibid., 177-178.

41 Tom Rockmore argues that "as Merleau-Ponty reads Lukács, Marx's concept of praxis provides the means to circumvent the sterile, bourgeois dichotomy between subjectivity and objectivity by revealing their possible future unity through the action of the proletariat." Tom Rockmore, "Merleau-Ponty, Marx, and Marxism: The Problem of History," *Studies in East European Thought* 48 (1996), 63-81, 76.

Lukács's dialectical interpretation of class-consciousness is crucial for Merleau-Ponty's reading of Marx in this essay and elsewhere. According to Merleau-Ponty, "Marxism is not a philosophy of the subject, but it is just as far from a philosophy of the object: it is a philosophy of history."[42] Here, he argues that existentialism shares with Marxism this historical orientation:[43]

> As its name suggests, existential philosophy consists of taking as one's theme not only knowledge [*connaissance*] or consciousness understood as an activity which autonomously posits immanent and transparent objects but also existence; i.e., an activity given to itself in a natural and historical situation and as incapable of abstracting itself from that situation as it is of reducing itself to it. Knowledge finds itself put back into the totality of human praxis and, as it were, given ballast by it. The 'subject' is no longer just the epistemological subject but it is the human subject who, by means of a continual dialectic, thinks in terms of his situation, forms his categories in contact with his experience, and modifies this situation and this experience by the meaning he discovers in them.[44]

While idealism posits consciousness as disjoined from the world and objective thought reduces consciousness to the world, existentialism approaches the subject of consciousness as dialectically embedded in its historical situation—i.e., as consciousness of that situation and as such, as practically engaged with and transformative of that situation. Knowledge is no longer confined to consciousness and divorced from embodied, situated and effective existence.[45] Instead, for existential philosophy, knowledge and praxis are indissolubly connected. What is crucial, then, is that the

42 Merleau-Ponty, "Marxism and Philosophy," 130.

43 "Society for man is not an accident he suffers but a dimension of his being. He is not in society as an object is in a box; rather, he assumes it by what is innermost in him" (Ibid., 128-129).

44 Ibid., 133-134.

45 "…man is a productivity, a relation to something other than himself, and not an inert thing. Shall we then define man as consciousness? This would still be a chimerical realization of the human essence, for once man is defined as consciousness, he becomes cut off from all things, from his body and his effective existence." Ibid., 129-130.

subject of existential-phenomenology is reconceived by Merleau-Ponty here as the subject of the materialist dialectic.[46]

4. Ethical Idealism and Liberal Ideology

This account of the materialist dialectic is at the heart of Merleau-Ponty's political philosophy in *Humanism and Terror*. Broadly speaking, Merleau-Ponty wrote this book as a response to the fraught historical and political situation of postwar geopolitical polarization and the pseudo-alternative this situation offered up to intellectuals in siding with either Soviet communism or American liberal capitalism. As he puts it in the preface,

> We find ourselves in an inextricable situation. The Marxist critique of capitalism is still valid and it is clear that anti-Sovietism today resembles the brutality, hybris [sic], vertigo, and anguish that already found expression in fascism. On the other side, the Revolution has come to a halt: it maintains and aggravates the dictatorial apparatus while renouncing the revolutionary liberty of the proletariat in the Soviets and its Party and abandoning the humane control of the state. It is impossible to be an anti-Communist and it is not possible to be a Communist.[47]

Merleau-Ponty argues that Arthur Koestler's famous critique of communism in *Darkness at Noon* (*Sonnenfinsternis,* 1940) as well as *The Yogi and the Commissar* (1945) is symptomatic of this situation, re-inscribing this pseudo-alternative on a conceptual plane. On one hand, Koestler conflates Marx's philosophy with Soviet communism. As such, Merleau-Ponty argues that Koestler's critique betrays a fundamental misunderstanding, reducing Marx's philosophy to what amounts to a deterministic, "mechanistic philosophy" that Koestler describes as a "philosophy of the Commissar."[48] From

46 "Man no longer appears as a product of his environment or an absolute legislator but emerges as a product-producer, the locus where necessity can turn into concrete liberty." Ibid., 134.

47 Maurice Merleau-Ponty, *Humanism and Terror* (Boston: Beacon, 1969), xxi.

48 "One is tempted to reply to Koestler that Marxism has actually transcended the alternative in which Rubashov loses himself. And indeed there

this misreading, Koestler accuses Marx of reducing consciousness vis-à-vis history. On Koestler's view, history operates in Marx's thought as an external force analogous to the causal determinacy of physical processes in the material world. Koestler thus mistakenly conflates Marx's philosophy of history with the metaphysical position of objective thought.[49] Standing opposed to the philosophy of the Commissar, is what Koestler describes as the "philosophy of the Yogi"—i.e., a purely spiritual and inward account of consciousness that is divorced from effective existence. The philosophy of the Yogi, for Koestler, signifies the abstract values of liberal humanism. Koestler seeks to reconcile this opposition; what he looking for, according to Merleau-Ponty, "is a 'synthesis' between the philosophy of the external which reduces everything to the framework of causal explanation, and the philosophy of the inward which confines itself to descriptions of the different levels of being and loses sight of their effective relations."[50] Yet what is missing from Koestler's analysis, he argues, is an understanding the materialist dialectic.[51] Such an analysis would reveal that the philosophy of the external and the philosophy of the inward are

is very little Marxism in *Darkness at Noon*...The solidarity of the individual with history which Rubashov and his comrades experienced in the revolutionary struggle gets translated into mechanistic philosophy which disfigures it and is the source of the inhuman alternatives with which Rubashov finishes." Ibid., 14.

49 "The whole [is] regarded as an assemblage of simple elements: life as a modality of physical nature, man as a modality of life, consciousness as a product or even an appearance—an homogenous world, stretched out flat without foreground or background; human action explained causally like any physical process; ethics and politics reduced to a utilitarian calculus; in a word, the total affirmation of the external." Ibid., 161.

50 Ibid., 163.

51 "But who has said that history is a clockwork and the individual a wheel? It was not Marx; it was Koestler. It is strange that in Koestler there is no inkling of the commonplace notion that by the very fact of its duration, history sketches the outline for the transformation of its own structures, changing and reversing its own direction because, in the last analysis, men come to collide with the structures that alienate them inasmuch as economic man is also a human being. In short, Koestler has never given much thought to the simple idea of dialectic in history." Ibid., 23.

both expressions of the failure to grasp the relationship between consciousness and history, between thought and its object, and between knowledge and praxis.

Pointing to the limits of Koestler's interpretation of Marx, Merleau-Ponty returns to the idea of the materialist dialectic. Crucially, what Koestler misses, he argues, is that this reconciliation of the subjective and objective can already be found in Marx's philosophy. Marx, following Hegel, has abandoned pure, abstract self-consciousness as the foundation of his philosophy in favor of taking up the position of situated, historical existence.[52] As Merleau-Ponty puts it:

> We only know of situated consciousnesses which blend themselves with the situation they take and are unable to complain at being identified with it or at the neglect of the incorruptible innocence of conscience. When one says that there is a history one means precisely that each person committing an act does so not only in his own name, engages not only himself, but also others whom he makes use of, so that as soon as we begin to live, we lose the alibi of good intentions; we are what we do to others, we yield the right to be respected as noble souls.[53]

Marxism, then, is not the "negation of subjectivity," a form of "scientific socialism," but rather "a theory of concrete subjectivity and concrete action—of subjectivity and action committed within a historical situation."[54] As such, Marx's philosophy also necessarily abandons the purity of abstract principles and values—the "original innocence" of pure consciousness along with the separation of theory and praxis.[55]

---

52 "…these are precisely the axioms that Marxism, following Hegel, questions by introducing the perspective of one consciousness upon another. What we find in the private life of a couple, or in a society of friends, or, with all the more reason, in history, is not a series of juxtaposed 'self-consciousnesses.' I never encounter face to face another person's consciousness any more than he meets mine. I am not for him nor is he for me a pure existence for itself. We are both for one another situated being, characterized by a certain way of treating other people and nature." Ibid., 108.

53 Ibid., 109.

54 Ibid., 22.

55 According to Merleau-Ponty, this view of the co-constitutive relation-

Without this understanding of the materialist dialectic, Merleau-Ponty argues that Koestler's critique of Soviet communism devolves into ideology. Here, he draws on Marx and Engels's claim in *The German Ideology* (*Die deutsche Ideologie*, 1945-1946) that ideological consciousness is an expression of the antagonisms of capitalist production. As Marx and Engels famously argue, "[c]onsciousness [*das Bewusstsein*] can never be anything else than conscious being [*das bewusste Sein*], and the being of men is their actual life-process."[56] If, as they claim, under the conditions of commodity production, human existence is structured by the fundamental antagonism that characterizes these productive relations, this antagonism is constitutive of consciousness and manifest in the form of ideology. In this sense, "[t]he phantoms formed in the brains of men are also, necessarily, sublimates of their material life-process."[57] The primary form that ideological consciousness takes, they argue, is that it views its own relationship to these material conditions precisely in an inverted form: the fact that consciousness is constituted by this socio-historical antagonism gives rise to the illusion of its transcendence and autonomy from these productive relations. As Marx and Engels put it:

> From this moment onwards consciousness can really flatter itself that it is something other than consciousness of existing practice, that it *really* represents something without representing something real; from now on consciousness is in a position to emancipate itself from the world and to proceed to the formation of

ship between consciousness and history, or understanding and effective existence underlies Marx's theory of class-consciousness: "it is not a matter of there being *both* an objective proletarian condition and an awareness of its condition which might be added to it gratuitously. The 'objective' condition itself induces the proletarian to become conscious of his condition, the very act of living that way motivates the awakening of consciousness." Ibid., 115.

56 Karl Marx and Friedrich Engels, *The German Ideology* (New York: Prometheus, 1998), 42. As Étienne Balibar puts it, "*The German Ideology* sets out an 'ontology of production' since, as Marx himself tells us, it is production which shapes *man's being*, to which he will oppose his consciousness: *Bewusst-sein*, literally his 'being conscious'." Étienne Balibar, *The Philosophy of Marx* (London: Verso, 2014), 35.

57 Marx and Engels, *The German Ideology*, 42.

'pure' theory, theology, philosophy, morality, etc.[58]

This ideological division of the material and ideal, they argue, is produced by and reflects the constitutive social antagonism of capitalism—i.e., that the reproduction of the bourgeois social order is compatible with the expression and realization of liberal-bourgeois values only in what Herbert Marcuse aptly describes as an "internalized and rationalized form."[59] According to Marcuse, this abstract and ideal sphere of liberal values, what Marx and Engels refer to as "pure theory, theology, philosophy, morality, etc.," is at once "essentially different from the factual world of daily struggle for existence, yet realizable by every individual for himself 'from within,' without any transformation of the state of fact."[60] Liberal-bourgeois values are thereby established beyond and outside of the existing conditions of life and simultaneously "democratized," invoked as accessible to all independently of the actual conditions of existence. Real, sensuous human beings invoke the value of freedom, equality and happiness that are available to them only in the abstract. The crucial point, for Marx and Engels, is that these abstractions reflect the material conditions that have produced them but in a distorted form.[61]

This critique of ideology is fundamental for Merleau-Ponty's treatment of liberal capitalism in *Humanism and Terror*. Here, he identifies the abstract consciousness of transcendental idealism as the consciousness of liberal bourgeois ideology. This abstract idealist philosophy of consciousness expresses the antagonism that separates the ideal from the material. As such, it represents the illusion of ideology, namely that, as Marx and Engels put it, "consciousness is something other than consciousness of existing practice."[62]

58 Ibid., 50.

59 Herbert Marcuse, *The Affirmative Character of Culture* (London: Mayfly, 2009), 73.

60 Ibid., 70.

61 What Balibar describes as "the dream of an impossible universality" that cannot be actualized in the current social order" Balibar, *The Philosophy of Marx*, 48.

62 Marx and Engels, *The German Ideology*, 50.

According to Merleau-Ponty, liberal capitalism appeals precisely to this subject of consciousness as the ground of its politics, invoking the principled non-violence of humanistic values in order to criticize the ostensibly violent means of Marxism.[63] As such, liberal capitalist societies appeal to the abstract ideals of freedom and equality apart from an analysis of material conditions within these societies, defending these abstract values, while at the same time dissimulating the violence of exploitation, oppression and subjugation that play a structural role in the material production and reproduction of life within capitalism.[64] On this basis, Merleau-Ponty argues that liberal humanism reflects the material conditions of existence and the relations of production, but in an inverted (i.e., ideological) form—the pure principles of its ethical idealism obfuscate the structural violence that is endemic to the relations of production.[65] As he put it, violence "in the liberal state, may be put outside the law, and, in effect, suppressed in the commerce of ideas though maintained in daily life in the form of colonization, unemployment, and wages."[66] It is therefore only on the basis of this ideological abstraction that liberal capitalism can present itself as the ally of universal freedom and equality, and violence as anathema.[67] By concealing the *de facto* violence of

---

63 Merleau-Ponty, however, rejects the claim that Marxism is tantamount to a form of realpolitik: "Marxism in principle denies any conflict between the exigencies of realism and those of ethics since the so-called 'ethics' of capitalism is a mystification, and the power of the proletariat is in reality what the bourgeois apparatus is only nominally. Marxism is no immorality but rather the determination not to consider virtues and ethics only in the heart of each man but also in the coexistence of men. The alternative between the actual and the ideal is transcended in the concept of the proletariat as the concrete vehicle of values." Merleau-Ponty, "Marxism and Philosophy," 125-126.

64 "Western humanism is a *humanism of comprehension*—a few mount guard around the treasure of Western culture; the rest are subservient" Merleau-Ponty, *Humanism and Terror*, 176.

65 As such, he insists that "the United States, with its anti-Semitism, racism, and strikebreaking, is only nominally the 'land of the free'." Ibid., 174.

66 Ibid., 103. He also insists that "the Revolution takes on and directs a violence which bourgeois society tolerates in unemployment and in war and disguises with the name of misfortune." Ibid., 107.

67 In *Capitalist Realism*, Mark Fisher describes the deflation of this

liberal capitalism, Merleau-Ponty argues that this form of ethical idealism in fact functions as a covert defense of bourgeois exploitation.[68]

The crucial claim, then, for Merleau-Ponty, is that to abandon idealist reflection is necessarily to abandon ethical idealism. Rather than abstract and unconditioned, what the dialectic introduces is an analysis of consciousness as the self-consciousness *of* these material conditions, i.e., self-consciousness of the conditions of commodity production. Consciousness is no longer simply on the side of the subject but passes over into the object and the object, in turn, incarnates consciousness. Consciousness is thereby disjoined not only from the abstract ideality but also thereby from the purity of ethical idealism. The implication, for Merleau-Ponty, is that we must cease "to judge liberalism in terms of the ideas it espouses and inscribes in constitutions" and rather demand "that these ideas be compared with the prevailing relations between men in the liberal state."[69] We can adequately assess liberal capitalism and actually existing communism only from the standpoint of this dialectical method.[70]

claim—from the lionization of liberal capitalism described by Merleau-Ponty to what Fisher describes as the "capitalist realism" of the late-twentieth and twenty-first century. Fisher invokes remarks by Alain Badiou to make this point: "partisans of the established order cannot really call [capitalism] ideal or wonderful. So instead, they have decided to say that all the rest is horrible. Sure, they say, we many not live in a condition of perfect Goodness. But we're lucky we don't live in a condition of Evil. Our democracy is not perfect. But it's better than the bloody dictatorships. Capitalism is unjust. But it's not criminal like Stalinism…" Mark Fisher, *Capitalist Realism* (London: Zero Book, 2009), 5.

68 In turn, the state socialism of the USSR justifies these violent means on the basis not only of its ostensibly non-violent ends but also on the basis of the de facto and extant violence of liberal-democracies. Within the USSR violence and deception have official status while humanity is to be found in daily life. On the contrary, in democracies the principles are human but deception and violence rule daily life." Merleau-Ponty, *Humanism and Terror*, 180.

69 Ibid., xiv.

70 As Merleau-Ponty argues, this shift: "puts the debate between the Western democracies and communism into its proper domain, which is not a debate between the Yogi and the Commissar but between one Commissar and another. If the events of the last thirty years lead us to doubt that the world pro-

5. Return of the Dialectic

There is an undeniable shift that occurs in Merleau-Ponty's treatment of Marxism between the publication of *Humanism and Terror* and *Adventures of the Dialectic*. By 1955, his earlier sympathy with the philosophy of Marx has been eroded by the events of the Korean War and his disillusionment with actually existing communism. In *Adventures of the Dialectic*, he is at times highly critical of Marx and yet he continues to question the relationship between Marx's philosophy and its contemporary iterations. What is consistent, however, between *Humanism and Terror* and *Adventures of the Dialectic* is Merleau-Ponty's commitment to a dialectical method. What we find in *Adventures of the Dialectic* is Merleau-Ponty's critique of the "ruin of the dialectic" vis-à-vis the "extreme objectivism" of revisionist Marxists, on one hand, and the "extreme subjectivism" of Sartre's "Ultrabolshevism," on the other.[71] Consequently, while he develops a critique of communism in *Adventures of the Dialectic*, he nevertheless attempts to retain the philosophical significance and critical force of the dialectic.

For Merleau-Ponty, the key to understanding the dialectic remains Marx's analysis of the commodity form in *Capital* and its interpretation in the work of Lukács. Here, as we saw in "Marxism and Philosophy," Merleau-Ponty draws once again on Marx's analysis of the peculiar ontological status of the commodity form, namely that it is a social relation between persons that appears in the form of a thing. Here he argues, once again, that with the rise of commodity production and the establishment of the commodity form as the universal category of social life, the peculiar onto-

letarian power in one country establishes reciprocal relations among men, they in no way affect the truth of that other Marxist idea that no matter how real and precious the humanism of capitalist societies may be for those who enjoy it, it does not eliminate unemployment, war, or colonial exploitation. Consequently, when set against the history of all men, like the freedom of the ancient city, it is the privilege of the few and not the property of the many. How do we answer the Indochinese or an Arab who reminds us that he has seen a lot of our arms but not much of our humanism?" Ibid., 175.

71 Merleau-Ponty, *Adventures of the Dialectic*, 98.

logical status of the commodity form impels a new philosophical method, one that reorients our understanding of the relationship between consciousness and matter, subject and object, and philosophy and history. Metaphysics is thereby supplanted by dialectic insofar as the object of inquiry must be understood as constituted rather than merely given and contemporary philosophical problems must be understood in reference their historical specificity, which within capitalist modernity means the socio-historical conditions of commodity production. As Merleau-Ponty puts it,

> This exchange, by which things become persons and persons things, lays the foundation for the unity of history and philosophy. It makes all problems historical but also all history philosophical, since forces are human projects become institutions. Capital, says Marx in a famous passage is "not a thing, but a social relationship between persons mediated by things (*nicht eine Sache, sondern ein durch Sachen vermitteltes gesellschaftliches Verhältnis zwischen Personen*)." Historical materialism is not the reduction of history to one of its sectors. It states a kinship between the person and the exterior, between the subject and the object, which is at the bottom of the alienation of the subject in the object and, if the movement is reversed, will be the basis for the reintegration of the world with man.[72]

Historical materialism, then, according to Merleau-Ponty, has nothing to do with economic reductivism but rather with the historical-philosophical critique of the commodity form. This critique of the commodity form institutes a dialectical approach to the categories and problems of history and philosophy insofar as critique is the self-consciousness of the commodity form itself.

In *Adventures of the Dialectic*, Merleau-Ponty argues that Lukács retains and develops this fundamental insight of Marx's philosophy. According to Merleau-Ponty, "Lukács is trying to preserve...a Marxism which incorporates subjectivity into history [*qui incorpore la subjectivité à l'historie*] without making it an epiphenomenon."[73] This means that consciousness is not simply

72 Ibid., 33.
73 Ibid., 41.

an epiphenomenon but neither is it abstract and unconditioned.[74] As Merleau-Ponty puts it, "What Lukács wishes to defend…is therefore always the idea that subjectivity is incorporated in history, not produced by it, and that history—generalized subjectivity, relationships among persons asleep and congealed in 'things'—is not an *in-itself*, governed, like the physical world, by causal laws, but is a totality to be understood."[75] Under the socio-historical condition of commodity production, consciousness is constituted by the commodity form and it is the self-consciousness of that form—i.e., the "self-consciousness of the object (*das Selbstbewusstsein des Gegenstandes*)."[76] Consciousness, Merleau-Ponty argues, thus refers to the "commodity seeing itself as commodity [*la merchandise s'apercevant comme merchandise*], [and] at the same time distinguishing itself from this, challenging the eternal laws of political economy, and discovering, under the supposed 'things,' the 'process' which they hide—that is to say, the dynamic of production, the social whole as 'production and reproduction of itself.'"[77]

For Lukács, the proletariat is defined as the self-consciousness of the commodity form. As such, the "polarized existence" of the proletariat—an existence that cannot be resolved into subject or object—constitutes the standard of truth, i.e., the model

74 Ibid., 40. "This results from a double relationship that an integral philosophy admits of between individuals and historical totality. It acts on us; we are in it at a certain place and in a certain position; we respond to it. But we also live it, speak about it, and write about it. Our experience everywhere overflows our standpoint. We are in it, but it is completely in us. These two relationships are concretely united in every life. Yet they never merge. They could be brought back to unity only in a homogeneous society where the situation would no more restrain life than life imprisons our gaze. All Marxism which does not make an epiphenomenon of consciousness inevitably limps, sometimes on one side, sometimes on the other." Ibid., 43

75 Ibid., 69. As he puts, it "For Lukács, [materialism] is a way of saying that all the relations among men are not the sum of personal acts or personal decisions, but pass through things, the anonymous roles, the common situations, and the institutions where men have projected so much of themselves that their fate is now played out outside of them." Ibid., 32.

76 Ibid., 45.

77 Ibid., 44-45.

of the relationship between subject and object.[78] On this model, the consciousness of the proletariat is neither simply ideologically determined by its material conditions nor does it transcend these conditions in a way that would provide consciousness with a synoptic view of history.[79] Truth is rather constituted by the "double relation or ambiguity of the dialectic [*la double rapport ou l'ambiguïté de la dialectique*]:" the ambiguity of the self-consciousness of the commodity form, the ambiguity of consciousness as constitutively embedded in history.[80] As such, the truth of the consciousness of the proletariat is inimical with a positivist view of the meaning or logic of history; the proletariat is not the truth of history in the sense of embodying an objectivist view of history as the necessary unfolding of a logical sequence of events. Rather, the consciousness of the proletariat refers to what Merleau-Ponty describes as the power of negation. As he states,

> Nothing is further from Marxism than positivistic prose: dialectical thought is always in the process of extracting from each phenomenon a truth which goes beyond it, waking at each moment our astonishment at the world and at history. This 'philosophy of history' does not so much give us the keys of history as it restores history to us as permanent interrogation [*interrogation permanente*]. It is not so much a certain truth hidden behind empirical history that it gives us; rather it presents empirical history as the genealogy of truth. It is quite superficial to say that Marxism unveils the meaning of history to us: it binds us to our time and its partialities; it does not describe the future for us; it does not stop our questioning—on the contrary it intensifies it. It

78 The proletariat "furnishes this identity of subject and object that philosophical knowledge perceives abstractly as the condition of truth and the Archimedes' point of a philosophy of history." Ibid., 45.

79 "Lukács rehabilitated consciousness in principle beyond ideologies but at the same time refused it the *a priori* possession of the whole...Most Marxists do exactly the opposite. They contest the existence of consciousness in principle and, without saying so, grant themselves the intelligible structure of the whole, and discover all the more easily the meaning and the logic of each phase in that they have dogmatically presupposed the intelligible structure of the whole." Ibid., 44.

80 Ibid., 69.

> shows us the present worked on by a self-criticism [*autocritique*], a power of negation and of sublation, a power which has historically been delegated to the proletariat.[81]

The proletariat, then, refers to the self-consciousness of the commodity form that is at the same time the interrogation of that form.[82] The truth that it grasps is not a positive reality beyond the given but rather the work of negation vis-à-vis the given.[83] This is why, for Merleau-Ponty, the dialectic ultimately refers to a method of permanent interrogation, i.e., the permanent self-interrogation of the given.

What Merleau-Ponty outlines in *Adventures of the Dialectic* as the "ruin of the dialectic" refers to those exegetes of Marx from Lenin to Sartre, who, he argues, reduce Marxism either to a philosophy of the object or subject.[84] According to Merleau-Ponty:

> The ruin of the dialectic is accomplished openly with Sartre and clandestinely with the communists, and the same decisions that the communists base on historical process and on the historical mission of the proletariat Sartre bases on the nonbeing of the proletariat and on the decision which, out of nothing, creates the proletariat as the subject of history.[85]

On one hand, actually existing communism invokes a mechanistic and determinist model of history as alibi, reducing the consciousness of the proletariat to an epiphenomenon. The dialectic as permanent interrogation is supplanted by historical necessity, and the critique of capitalism devolves into ideology. On the other hand, Merleau-Ponty argues that in *The Communists and Peace* (*Les Communistes et la Paix*, 1952-1954) Sartre disjoins consciousness from history such that the consciousness of the proletariat ultimately appears as spontaneous and unconditioned, and history as a product

81 Ibid., 56-57.

82 Ibid., 44-45. See above.

83 See, for example, Diana Coole's reading of Merleau-Ponty's critique of rationalism in *Merleau-Ponty and Modern Politics after Anti-Humanism*.

84 Barry Cooper describes this as a "fracturing of the dialectic into consciousness and things." Cooper, *Merleau-Ponty and Marxism*, 131.

85 Merleau-Ponty, *Adventures of the Dialectic*, 98.

of volition.[86] As he puts it, "[o]ne feels that for Sartre the dialectic has always been an illusion…Marxist action has always been pure creation."[87] The problem, then, as Merleau-Ponty argues, is that both subjectivism and objectivism annul the critical force of the dialectic insofar as it is the ambiguity of consciousness and history—i.e., the ambiguity of the self-consciousness *of* history—that constitutes the dialectic as permanent interrogation. To resolve this ambiguity in favor of the subjective or objective is to abolish the dialectic itself.

What the materialist dialectic in fact presents in an asymmetrical negation, i.e., destruction without the generation of a positive supplement to fill in the gap of what it destroys. That is, the dialectic cannot be understood as a negation that simply generates a new, positive identity in its place. As he argues, "[w]hat then is obsolete is not the dialectic but the pretension of terminating it in an end of history, in a permanent revolution, or in a regime which, being the contestation of itself, would no longer be contested from the outside and, in fact, would no longer have anything outside it."[88] The proletariat as the subject of materialist politics does not constitute a positive identity, a universal class that would take the place of a structural class-antagonism. Rather the proletariat, as we have seen, refers only to the peculiar ontological status that belongs to the self-consciousness of the commodity form (*l'autoconnaissance de la merchandise*, i.e., *l'autoconnaissance de l'objet*).[89] It is in this sense that the class-consciousness of the proletariat is just the self-consciousness of history, which is to say, history as permanent self-interrogation. The materialist dialectic thus remains critical and transformative not because it appeals to a position outside of history's self-consciousness of itself but because the asymmetrical structure of negation preserves the place of opposition.[90] As

86 Ibid., 97-98.

87 Ibid., 98.

88 Ibid., 206.

89 Maurice Merleau-Ponty, *Les adventures de la dialectique* (Paris: Gallimard, 1955), 62-63.

90 Barry Cooper offers a similar interpretation of the dialectic. See

such, the proletariat is neither the subject nor the object of politics but rather marks the constitutive ambiguity of the dialectic that cannot be resolved in these terms.

Cooper, *Merleau-Ponty and Marxism*, 131-133.

DISTINCTION, PARTICIPATION, AND EMPTY EMBODIMENT

ADAM LOVASZ

When even the seer is revealed as a ubiquity of non-selves, a collection of flesh and blood molecules, an assemblage characterized, like anything else in and of the world, by dependent co-arising, then the very sense of life is transformed from a mode of individuality into a collectivity. Our lives are characterized by a strange entanglement with death. No superiority has precedence over the elemental. The elemental is a perturbation, incompatible with any ontological hierarchy. Dependent arising (*paṭiccasamuppāda*) means, first and foremost, that change, in itself, is incomprehensible. Everything is dependent upon something else. The concepts through which we interpret the world are never commensurate with relations themselves. There is no such thing as a change of state or composition in and of itself; there is no motion prior to the mover's commencement of movement: "Whatever motion in terms of which a mover is spoken of, he does not move by that motion. Because he does not exist prior to motion, who or what is it that moves?" asks Nagarjuna, the founder of Madhyamaka Buddhism.[1] Outside of dependent arising, there can be no power or, indeed, any existence in itself. Aside from relations there is nothing.[2] Empirically speaking, this means that while relations do exist

1 Nagarjuna, *Mūlamadhyamakakārikā of Nagarjuna*, trans. David J. Kalupahana (Delhi: Motilal Banarsidass, 1999), 130.

2 Jane Bennett, *Vibrant Matter. A Political Ecology of Things* (Durham: Duke University Press, 2010).

within the world, and have a certain relative reality, they nonetheless lack any substantial basis: reality, for Nagarjuna, is merely conventional, never substantial.[3] It is not enough to say that everything is composed of multiple flows or multiplicities. Rather, the movements themselves are inseparable from that which moves. But the mover itself is also nothing but a surface effect of other entities. And so on, *ad infinitum.* An infinity of movement meets with an abyssal entanglement of entanglements, without end. And yet we see multitudes, we as creatures endowed with vision have eyes able to enjoy saturated visual fields. Nothing lies outside of the perturbations, there is no unchanging, eternal ego-self that would see all of this. If we accept the mutual interdependence of all there is, "we"—whatever it is that perceives, whatever evolutionary tendencies or genetic structures that compose that which calls itself a "self"—come to understand that the world, for all its liveliness and tonality, is "a very colourful nothing."[4] If visualization pertains to nothing more than this colourful nothingness, negation too, even the most destructive of aggressions, can be no more than small dots of overflowing emotion, colliding with the vengeful organism's neighborhood.

Visualization is the practice of coming into contact with an Outside whose content nevertheless determines, even at times

---

3 Whether this makes Nagarjuna a "nihilist" in any Western sense of the word is an irrelevant issue, as is whether "nihilism" as a broadly defined semantic construct applies to Nagarjuna's ontology. Ontology always transcends the scope of mere philological semantics. What matters is that we recognize the full ontological implications of negating the substantial reality of all relations. The concept of dependent origination entails the rejection of any preconventional, preconceptual basis for existence. As Jay Garfield writes, "dependent origination simply is the explicability and coherence of the universe. Its emptiness is the fact that there is no more to it than that." According to the tenets of relational ontology, there is nothing more to relations than their own, promiscuous, inscrutable givenness. What is relevant from our perspective is the "nothing more" of co-arising, mutually neutralizing phenomena. Jay Garfield, "Dependent Arising and the Emptiness of Emptiness: Why Did Nagarjuna Start with Causation?," *Philosophy East and West*, 44.2 (1994), 227.

4 Jimmy Pianka, "Colourful Nothing: Emptiness in the Madyamaka," *Aporia* 19.2 (2009): 33-44.

undermines, our own sense of having a self. Our constitution is rendered amenable to change, to penetration. What is passivity, if not a usage made of our corporeality that reduces this body we have to a state of selfless shatteredness? The dilemma we hope to capture is the question of what ontology can make of passivity, sexual passivity included. What can philosophy make of the state of non-action? All illusions of grandeur and omnipotence melt away once the immensity of the world collides with our impotence. Differences in scale seem to beckon toward acceptance, while rejection tends to be produced by negative molecular constitutions, microscopic parasitical affects that feed upon weakness, desire and resentment. A recent study has highlighted the connection between Borderline Personality Disorder (BPD) and a high sensitivity to injustice.[5] Could it be that the unavoidable inequality of reality itself poses a threat to the subject's sense of integrity? It is painful, almost unbearable to even think of the various iniquities prevalent within the world. At the most elemental level, reality is pervaded by force, violence and destruction. Alphonso Lingis puts it well when he writes the following: "birth is discontinuity, unreason, and violence."[6] Nothing would be more comforting than to envision a world without these three. But the fact of the matter is that these multitudes of molecular forces, dark crevices and mutually inseparable pollutions are always already composed in a manner so as to produce collisions, forceful explosions of activity giving birth to new becomings. Hierarchy is not quite the correct concept; in evolution, one cannot speak of more advanced forms or manifestations. Each corporeality is adapted to respond to another. Drawing upon Amotz Zahavi's idea of the "handicap principle", Geoffrey Miller has proposed a theory of display production that highlights the role of prodigious waste in sexual selection.[7] How-

5 Stefanie Lis, Anna Schaedler, Lisa Liebke, Sophie Hauschild, Janine Thome, Christian Schmahl, Dagmar Stahlberg, Niko Kleindienst, and Martin Bohus, "Borderline personality disorder features and sensitivity to injustice," *Journal of Personality Disorders* (2017): 1-15.

6 Alphonso Lingis, *Body Transformations. Evolutions and Atavisms in Culture* (New York and Abingdon: Routledge, 2005), 4.

7 Amotz Zahavi, *The Handicap Principle. A Missing Piece of Darwin's Puzzle*

ever non-sexual some visual displays may appear, a sexual function need not necessarily be apparent to any of the participants in a process of courtship. However, displays must have high information value, and this is guaranteed by none other than the wastefulness of their production: "prodigious waste is a necessary feature of sexual courtship. Peacocks as a species would be much better off if they did not have to waste so much energy growing big tails. But as individual males and females, they have irresistible incentives to grow the biggest tails they can afford, or to choose sexual partners with the biggest tails they can attract. In nature, showy waste is the only guarantee of truth in advertising."[8] Signals are self-referential, in the sense that they are designed to draw other bodies closer to us, allowing for a blending of corporealities. But such communication can only be effective if it is accompanied by an inordinate, irrational waste of our energies, even to the point of death and dissolution. Bodily realities, just like any other levels of the world, are mutually dependent. One needs another, willing body, a body in heat, in order for a sexually selected signal to operate effectively. Signalling is the production of expensive, wasteful molecular dispositions and constitutions that render a body accessible to another, an Other whose outside strips it of the veneer of its impenetrability. This mutual interblending cannot be reduced to phallocentric notions of penetration, for sexual union is an interpenetration, a breaking open of the world's shell so as to extract nutritional values.

The world of inhabitation is a place of hospitality, and is thus always open to multiple usages. No single entity can lay claim to the entirety of signals. Even the greediest of female redback spiders cannot consume all of the males foolhardy enough to approach her. Up to 65% of matings end in the cannibalization of the male by the female.[9] Does this in any way invalidate our claim,

(Oxford: Oxford University Press, 1997); Geoffrey Miller, *Spent. Sex, Evolution, and Consumer Behavior* (New York and London: Penguin Books, 2009)

8 Geoffrey Miller, "Waste is Good", last modified February 20, 1999. https://www.prospectmagazine.co.uk/magazine/wasteisgood

9 Maydianne Andrade CB, "Risky mate search and male self-sacrifice in redback spiders," *Behavioral Ecology* 14.4 (2003): 531-538.

made just moments ago, that the world is a place of hospitality? What is hospitality anyway? Is the female spider not hospitable in her openness to courtship and genetic renewal? She functions as an ocean of disappearance, an all-consuming vagina that nevertheless allows certain intrepid specimens to escape from her jaws. The fact that 65% of males are consumed during intercourse also entails that 35% nevertheless find a way to escape their fate. Is this not in itself cause for celebration? Nutrition and reproduction, two vectors that necessitate an inextricable involvement with risk, danger, and awful contingency. Meaning signals to us: here is a plenitude operating at the outermost spaces of risky embodiment, an opening within Being that could allow the memes manipulating our senses to continue their proliferation in space and time. When we refer to something repeatedly, we intend to mean the same thing, but this intention must, of necessity, fail to reach its destination. Selection necessitates the inference of a closure that would prevent the accomplishment of any finality. Closure is inseparable from repetition, for closure attests to the imperishable ontological relief that is multiplicity. "Pain", explains Leo Bersani, "is the organism's protection against self-dissolution."[10] In sexual excess, however, as exemplified by sadomasochistic enjoyment, "the ego renounces its power over the world."[11] Again, we have here a passivity that refuses to blend with the Outside. Masochistic enjoyment is the pain we desire to feel, the painful sense of having a body rendered open to laceration, and orifices fatally unable to become re-enclosed. Pain is the movement of a body that would return to a state of self-referential closure with regard to its environs. But excess already forecloses any and all descriptions that would restore a phallocentric, logocentric rational Occidental male subjectivity.

Multiplicity, including the multiplicity of perversions and strange sexual practices, is truly astonishing. During the course of 2017, scientists observed several instances of Japanese snow monkeys having sexual relations with sika deer. Not only males

10 Leo Bersani, *Homos* (Cambridge, Mass.: Harvard University Press, 1996), 94.

11 Bersani, *Homos*, 94-5.

specimens, but also female monkeys used the deer for their own enjoyment, oblivious to supposed species boundaries. This behavior, the researchers surmised, constituted what could be thought of as a "new behavioral tradition."[12] What drove the young females to ride the backs of adult deer and rub their clitorises into their manes? What is it about the form of a deer that transforms this, for us, innocuous creature, into an object of perverse desire, a tool for erogenous exploration or masturbation? It was thought that the monkeys engaged in these activities must have been outcasts, social renegades. But such a functional explanation, we feel, cannot really get to the heart of the matter. Forms and relations, after reaching a certain point of development, seem to fragment into newer becomings. Anything that is accomplishable tends to be accomplished. If young female monkeys are able to jump upon the backs of male sika deer—and the latter do not back away from such interspecies encounters—then so they shall. Their sexual excitement will be enacted through perversion. The accomplishable cannot be stopped by supposed species boundaries—warmth seeks after warmth. In the cold climate, any warm body can become an object of sexual frenzy, a hospitable source of stimulation. As Luce Irigaray reminds us, "we haven't been taught, nor allowed, to express multiplicity. To do that is to speak improperly."[13] Whether one speaks of multiplicity in sexual selection, or in political terms, or in the context of a mundane setting, it is always astonishing, always a mesmerizing display of colourful nothingness that never ceases to surprise. Novelty never seems to quite wear off. The multiple is that which elides differentiations of inside and outside, this and that, Self and Other. But multiplicity is also the embodiment of difference. When young female snow monkeys ride male deer, they are embodying themselves in ways that surprise human observers, and perhaps even other monkeys. Deposited within every

12 Nicola Davis, "Sex between snow monkeys and sika deer may be 'new behavioral tradition'", last modified December 15, 2017, https://www.theguardian.com/science/2017/dec/15/sex-between-snow-monkeys-and-sika-deer-may-be-new-behavioural-tradition

13 Luce Irigaray, *This Sex Which Is Not One*, trans. Catherine Porter and Carolyn Burke (Ithaca, NY.: Cornell University Press, 1985), 209.

living thing is a multiplicity of molecular forces, energies that form the basis of any ontogenesis. Encompassing speech and communication is a visibility that beckons toward activity, even at the expense of self-shattering annihilation. Bersani invites us to imagine "a nonsuicidal disappearance of the subject", a contradiction in terms if there ever was one.[14] This contradiction need not be conceived of as something necessitating immediate correction, as if bodies were ever meant to be regulated by words or philosophical concepts. Corporeality is capable of extreme divergence: neither speech, nor bodily materiality may be conceived of as being completely independent of one another. Interdependence means, first and foremost, the exclusion of any solitary view. All things are entwined within relations. In fact, they are the relations they unite within their folds.

Every enclosure demands a commensurate inner openness; borders are predicated upon a multiplicity of productive inner worlds sacrificing their energies for the maintenance of the assemblage they enact. Myriam Kyselo has proposed a model of the self as an autonomous enactive interpersonal system. In the enactivist model, cognition is not a passive reception of environmental stimuli, but rather an interactive interface with an environment that produces meaning: "Cognitive individuation in the autonomous self-production of identity entails a view of cognition as goal-directed, value-driven and purposeful. Cognitive systems have a basic intrinsic twofold goal: to create and maintain an identity and to generate sense or meaning."[15] Enactivism means that selves are inherently relational, not in spite of their autonomy, but precisely because of the autonomy of their self-production. The body is the ground of cognition, an anonymity that, through various cultural practices, nevertheless becomes our own. This leg, this anus, this mouth, this set of eyes we have are ours, but can also, at least potentially, become those of others as well. Even complete strangers may lay claim to certain body parts of ours. Not infrequently in

14 Bersani, *Homos*, 99.

15 Miriam Kyselo, "The Body Social: An Enactive Approach to the Self." *Frontiers in Psychology* 5, (2014): 6.

many countries, organs are removed from dead hospital patients and executed convicts without any legal consent from surviving relatives. Cognitive development is a ripening of our developmental stages, a heightening of our awareness to signals, cues, codes, symbols, attractions and displays. The world would be unnavigable, incomprehensible, were it not for the various signs we find ourselves surrounded with. The world—our world, as well as that of others—is full of signs, signposts pointing toward hidden machineries, divinely ordained or otherwise. What use one body can make of another is always inherently determined by its own constitutive possibilities, its mutational capabilities. Mysteriously, multiplicity also manifests itself in the display of purposelessness. Not all displays can be readily assigned a biological function. Sometimes, machineries intended for the ejection of waste are reversed. Enactment can be turned inside out; the Outside then arrives within a mouth, smeared upon a tongue hungry for the taste of excrement: "every organ coupling and, by an anaclitic deviation, be turned to the production of erotogenous surfaces: the mouth can draw in nutriment but also slaver, drool, google, and babble; the anus can release excrement but also spread it into a surface of warm pleasure."[16] Once surfaces are transformed into erotogeneous opportunities, enactment runs rampant and maladaptation becomes so much more than a merely negative form of failure. As soon as the powers of suppression and self-restriction are diverted into the enjoyment of perversity, bodies learn to bleed with matter.

Enactment progressively merges with an inorganic environment. Misperception can invite death, as when an animal falls off a cliff or a mountain climber falls into a glacier and freezes. Where some bodies bleed, other are preparing to lay claim to their interiorities. What is maladaptation? What is perversion? All phenomena, we must remember, are dependent upon one another. According to the relational view, there is no such thing as a thing in itself. There is no self outside of the realm of intersubjectivity. Even when we are alone, this solitude is a thing that gains its ontological status from the *absence* of other subjects. Solitude is, strictly

16 Lingis, *Body Transformations*, 61.

speaking, impossible. Nobody is alone. But then again, nobody is truly anybody: togetherness proves just as impossible. Logically speaking, it is inconsistent to accept the ontological circumstance of mutual dependence without also accepting the impossibility of collectivity, at least in a substantial sense. Simply put, if there are no parts in themselves, there can be no whole they compose. But what then of those undeniably colourful phenomena, those displays that dot the landscape and almost compel our senses, through the powers of allure they emanate? What should we make of the peacock's tail? The male bird is surely oblivious to such abstract matters as philosophy. All phenomena are dependent upon their interrelations, the more or less dense ecologies they inhabit. Here we propose a concept that could serve as a bridge between various living organisms engaged in relations of mutual attraction, without compromising our nondualistic ontological commitment to the ultimate emptiness of each and every existing (and nonexistent) thing. This bridging concept we call, following Christopher Groves, the "anticipatory assemblage."[17] Allure would be an ontological condition of mutuality, in which participants enact each other's agency by occupying places within a larger relation of anticipation that transcends their individuality. Excess is, above all else, made possible by the elemental need of perceivers to extend themselves through time toward another point, a future environment. Anticipation is a characteristic of organisms endowed with cognitive capabilities, organic beings able not only to respond to stimuli but also to construe new environments of their own. Self-production is a universal characteristic of all that lives. Awakening constitutes the point of departure, an invitation to engage in exploring multiple folds, freeing ripples of illicit pleasures, enjoyments. Each enjoyment is a death, a luxurious expenditure that opens the organism to an Outside that is always already relative to the body's interiority. All phenomena, in this moment of openness, are here, at once, as if summoned by a natural magic. This flesh, in the here and now of emergent emancipation, is a non-melting tex-

17 Christopher Groves. "Emptying the future: On the environmental politics of anticipation," *Futures* 92 (2017): 33.

ture, whose fullness is derived from the alternation of its softening and hardening. Once the blood rushes forth amongst its vessels, the penis hardens, while the same event has the opposite effect on the vagina or anus: that which accepts the power of invitation is no longer a mere passive emptiness, but likewise an active participant in union, even if the entire chaotic scene of sexual release occurs within a passive, empty *contexture*. All relations in and of the world are empty, without final substance. But does this in any way deter lovers from sinking into each other's non-melting flesh? Following Hans Jonas, Kyselo identifies an inner tension within organic life. On the one hand, beings are dependent upon material resources, nourishing flows emerging from a hospitable environment. On the other hand, that which lives is also characterized by "a striving for emancipation" from that very environment.[18] Jonas captures this tension with the phrase "needful freedom", a concept that may also be linked with operational closure.[19] Bodies are social because they interface with their environs, but simultaneously must also remain closed to the various forces surrounding them, otherwise the chaos of the Outside instantiates a complete dissolution of the organism. If bodies are interfaces, this necessarily implies that they are more than mere semantic operations, words embedded within material contexts, or a Nous, an intelligence whose language works itself upon an otherwise passive landscape.

Wasteful forms of non-reproductive sexuality are, for Georges Bataille, inescapably linked with death: "eroticism is assenting to life even in death."[20] Death does not mean the end of sexuality; only the essentialism of a culture predicated upon the continuous denial of negation and the negative can obscure the suchness of the dark underworld underlying corporeality. Is a Buddhist notion of the machinic possible? What is the machinic, as opposed to the thickness of embodied experience? To better grasp

18 Kyselo, "The Body Social", 5.

19 Ibid; Humberto Maturana and Francisco Varela, *The Tree of Knowledge. Understanding the Biological Roots of Human Understanding.* (Boston: Shambala Publications, 1992)

20 Georges Bataille, *Erotism. Death and Sensuality*, trans. Mary Dalwood (San Francisco: City Lights Books, 1986), 11.

these questions, let us further elaborate upon the concept of anticipatory assemblages already introduced above. When it recedes from the view of living perceivers, the sensible does not melt away into an invisible nothingness. As the potential for visibility, it remains everpresent within landscapes. The sensible is an order of being that extends across the dual realm of visibility and invisibility. Events taking place within the sensible redouble in the form of memories and stored potentials, within the context of fundamentally heterogeneous structures. According to Groves' broad definition, anticipation refers "to the capacity of an organised system to incorporate projected future states into its present functioning, as a way of orienting or modulating its activity."[21] Events are never pure exteriorities, hence the nonsensicality of economic theories that define the environment of an economic system in such terms. Anticipation is the ability of any non-trivial system, living or otherwise, to modulate its operations in reference to future events, probabilities and uncertainties. Decisions are not the exclusive prerogative of human actants, because several different materialities affect the outcomes of even seemingly human-oriented political, economic or social acts. The social cannot be conceived of as a clear-cut dichotomy between individual bodies and social institutions, human intentions and material realities. As materially and corporeally embedded bodies, human minds are also dependent upon the cognitive redoubling of various material factors. Anything from a pleasant spring day to the infection of our computer by ransomware spreading through cyberspace can affect our mood, painting it in various hues, provoking gulps, faster breaths or erotic sensations. A 2005 study found that mild spring weather, typically referred to as "good" weather, can temporarily broaden cognitive capabilities in humans.[22] Hence moods and emotions too have an ecology, as well as a temporality. Emotions are temporal phenomena that crossover into our bodies from outside, only to be

21 Groves, "Emptying the Future", 30.

22 Matthew C. Keller, Barbara L. Fredrickson, Oscar Ybarra, Stéphane Côté, Kareem Johnson, Joe Mikels, Anne Conway, and Tor Wager, "A warm heart and a clear head: The contingent effects of weather on mood and cognition," *Psychological science* 16.9, (2005): 724-731.

ejected again by either opposing passions, cravings, or some transcendental meditation, designed to disrupt and suspend the passions. Death also has an atmosphere, even a contagiousness which makes it imperative that we hide the bodies of the deceased in tombs or even reduce them to ashes blown away by the gusts of a cruel wind. The weather too is endowed with emotions, concerns, excitements, and enticements. When the sun expends its warmth upon the surface of Earth, genitals become more active, whereas in winter, the locus of excitement shifts to the warm fireplace, if at all (humans are among the few animals whose sexual escapades are not locked into the alternation of the seasons). Glamour and allure are but the superficial sides of a deeper reality, the reality of abjection, pollution, impurity. "The fascination with glamour", Lingis writes, "ends in a muck of steamy breath, vaginal fluids, semen, and blood."[23] Every enjoyment is a joyful shattering of self, a return to anonymous, formless materiality. Erotic relations are body transformations, to borrow the title of Lingis' book, deconstructions of thickness tantamount to a potentially infinite laceration of self and other. Alterity, once it comes into proximity with brutal phenomena, can only be removed at the cost of becoming an absolutely residual, sticky substance, not quite fluid and not quite solid, a goo. Even after the most thrilling of sexual encounters, we cannot help feeling that something has been lost, a mystery has been profaned, fluids have gone to waste, and energy has been expended. Death, like sex, is a disorder, a chaos that explodes the sphere of work and productive utility like some final *kenosis*, with the notable exception that this apocalypse recurs again and again... Eroticism differs from the realm of the everyday; not unlike death, it reintroduces mysterious discontinuities into temporality.[24]

That which is lost never exists independently of the conditions of its disappearance. Neither presence, nor absence may be derived from themselves. Similarly, the body as a social unit is not entirely self-sufficient. Autonomy does not entail a hermetic separation from one's own lifeworld. Quite the contrary: autonomy,

23 Lingis, *Body Transformations*, 36.
24 Bataille, *Erotism*, 46.

defined as partial separation, seclusion, is built upon a prior embeddedness within a world that always precedes our desires for emancipation. Beings and organizations alike are intrinsically purposeful, even if at times they also have a need for shedding their purposes, grand plans and goals in favour of aimless debauchery or perversion or simply time-wasting activities. Kyselo extends the idea of needful freedom, transferring it from the level of individual biological entities to social relations in general. Hence the body, as a social assemblage, is an identity selectively open, through various mechanisms of distinction, taste, and identification, to the needs and desires of the alterities surrounding it. In the enactive framework, the self is no longer thought of as being equated with either a disembodied mind, or an individuated body, but rather is conceptualized as a "self-other-generated network."[25] Both self and other affect the growth of new corporealities. We must remain perpetually vigilant against the double temptation to reduce bodies to social and/or biological constructs. Levi R. Bryant's notion of the machinic can be of help in this regard: "a machine is a system of operations that perform transformations on inputs thereby producing outputs."[26] If we think of the social body, as defined by Kyselo's enactivist view, as a machinic entity, a product of anticipatory assemblages encoding society, then we may avoid the hazards of reductionist approaches to corporeality. The body would then be a materiality dependently arising from various social operations, while also becoming, through the process of its individuation, ever more able to select inputs from its environment. Every being is a machine, in the sense that it selects energies from a certain ecological contexture, and ejects forces into that very same ecology, contributing to transformative events. Inasmuch as they operate as anticipatory assemblages, societies and bodies alike introduce abstract patterns, empty futures into phase spaces influenced by their unit operations. Machines, if and when they operate in a non-trivial manner, are liable to producing "anticipatory represen-

25 Kyselo, "The Body Social", 9.

26 Levi R. Bryant, *Onto-Cartography. An Ontology of Machines and Media* (Edinburgh: Edinburgh University Press, 2014), 38.

tations", in order to better orient themselves and give directions for future actions and movements.[27] Every machine has some kind of purpose, even if that purpose may often be misinterpreted in terms of the absolute lack of one. Anticipation coils up within the machine, until the time of exertion arrives, until the point wherein the body must learn to make an effort and enact a transformation. That which operates according to principles of self-organization has one imperative: create a transformation, make a change, enact your self. Here, within the self-other-generated network, unprecedented intimacy exists alongside the possibility of incalculable frigidity. Integrity and dissolution are two sides of subjectivity, two poles between which resides the subject as an inevitable, unavoidable choice. Living beings and organizations, as opposed to mere automatons, must always choose between their integrity and the shattering of self-sufficiency. Autonomy means the ever-present potentiality of self-dissolution. Distinction means "emancipation from others", whereas openness involves "participation."[28] Taken to their extremes, both distinction and participation lead to the death of the social self. Absolute separation, as in the case of solitary confinement, ruptures the relations of the confined individual, while complete openness destroys the agent's borderlines, ruining the integrity of their inner structures.

When the machinic body shatters, when the self-rupturing event occurs, how are we to react to the shock of real disembodiment and dismemberment? It could be mentioned that we have devoted too much of our attention to merely erotic transgression. There are instances of absolute participation that explode the self in a quite literal sense, without thereby necessarily demolishing the social self. Namely, we are thinking here of the suicide bomber. Analyzing dramatic U.S. media representations of female suicide bombers in U.S.-occupied Iraq in the early 21st century, Marita Gronnvoll and Kristen McCauliff interpret such accounts in terms of abjection. Veiled Muslim women who use fake pregnancies to smuggle explosive devices into crowded, otherwise secure areas

27 Groves, "Emptying the Future", 33.
28 Kyselo, "The Body Social", 10-11.

represent the ultimate insult to gender norms and stereotypes, for the female body is supposed to be a life-giving source of plenitude: "their bodies, so particularly diseased and polluted, escape their seemingly secure confinement, and become a deadly weapon of mass destruction not only to their owners, but to everyone else. (...) Women who fake pregnancy to such nefarious ends as taking life rather than giving life demonstrate that the abject is never truly under control."[29] The bodies of suicide bombers are bodies that shatter, while leaving behind traces in the form of martyred social selves, uploaded onto terrorist websites, idolized by their surviving relatives or vilified by the enemy's media. What the suicide bomber displays is the staggering potentiality latent within self-shattering practices. Without seeking to ethically justify such brazen acts of political and religious violence, the image of a body willingly sacrificing itself has an element of wastefulness that literally beggars belief. It cannot be the case that social death can be entirely equated with absolute participation within a destructive, fiery flux, for these men (and women) who die for their communities survive their own self-shattering experiences in the form of socially instituted martyr-iconographies.[30] They participate in networks of religious and political meaning long after they have been dismembered, strewn across the street of a Green Zone, along with the scattered remains of victims both guilty and innocent. Bodies that shatter defy both binary codes of differentiation and the ontological lines of division separating activity from passivity, self and other. Could we postulate a middle point between absolute distinction and complete participation, a stage wherein both melt into one another? This would be the space of absolute freedom, the degree zero of both autonomy and life. A life lived for another would bleed into a death dealt upon oneself that opens a horrifying, nauseatic hole within space-time, detonating the temporal

29 Marita Gronnvoll, and Kristen McCauliff, "Bodies that Shatter: A Rhetoric of Exteriors, the Abject, and Female Suicide Bombers in the 'War on Terrorism,'" *Rhetoric Society Quarterly* 43.4 (2013): 346.

30 Frances S. Hasso, "Discursive and political deployments by/of the 2002 Palestinian women suicide bombers/martyrs," *feminist review* 81.1 (2005): 23-51.

continuum. Acts of spectacular, undifferentiating violence are the polar opposites of anything that may be termed nutritional, hence the terror evoked by the unlikely figure of females smuggling explosives under the pretense of a non-existent pregnancy. Productive life would henceforth become the object of unlimited suspicion. A particularly melodramatic newspaper article captures the sheer irrationality of the communication that may be unleashed by such destructive corporeality: "Female Bombers Spread Terror; Iraqis Grow Wary of Women."[31] The female suicide bomber damages the borders between male and female, activity and passivity, integrity and dissolution in ways that more conventional male suicide attackers cannot seem to achieve. The explosive feminine is a deadly potentiality that comes to matter through the productivity of its absent presence.

Even if our examples may seem indulgent, at times autotelic, this should not detract from the ethical imperative we seek to advance. Namely, we have striven to show embodiment as a fundamentally social and enacted agency. Running across corporeality is the troubling duality of distinction and participation. As we have hoped to show through various examples, these two categories, coalescing in the idea of socially needful freedom, have a tendency to interpenetrate one another. The corporeal cannot be separated from the social or the material. Indeed, as the materiality of anticipation shows, even emotions are never entirely subjective components of the world, but also medial tracings of environmental factors. Every kind of weather corresponds with a certain kind of mood, and each mood has a particular type of weather pattern most adequate to its proliferation. Lastly, we have attempted to show that limitless participation need not entail the complete destruction of the social self, for martyrdom can easily allow a certain form of iconic subjectivity to survive the complete dismemberment of a body that shatters.

31 Gronnvoll and McCauliff, "Bodies that Shatter", 348.

EMBODIED EXPERIENCE OF MULTIPLICITOUS SELFHOOD

Mariana Ortega's Latina Feminist Phenomenology

MARIANA ORTEGA INTERVIEWED BY
JULIAN EVANS, JESSICA ELLIS, AND SANGIE ZAITSOFF

Mariana Ortega is Associate Professor of Philosophy and Women's, Gender and Sexuality Studies at Pennsylvania State University and the author of In-Between: Latina Feminist Phenomenology, Multiplicity, and the Self *(2016). Ortega brings an original approach to questions of selfhood and identity by intertwining the work of Latina feminists such as Gloria Anzaldúa and María Lugones with existential phenomenology, in particular the work of Martin Heidegger. Understanding the self as both singular and multiple, Ortega examines accounts of world-traveling and border crossings that illuminate the everyday experiences of marginality, migration, and exile. With keen attention to the experience of living between worlds and the borders that define—politically and conceptually—current categories of identity, Ortega's work challenges abstract and general accounts of selfhood that remain central to the academic tradition of philosophy, a tradition that has marginalized and ignored the unique contributions of Latina feminists and other theorists of colour who deeply understand the experience of being-between-worlds.*

The Centre for the Study of Theory and Criticism hosted Professor Ortega as a guest speaker on March 16th, 2018, where she gave a lecture entitled "Altars for the Living: Shadow Ground, Aesthetic Memory, and the US/Mexico Borderlands." This forceful talk dug into aesthetic reactions and reflections to the ongoing humanitarian crisis taking place at the US/Mexico border. Following the talk, Professor Ortega was interviewed by three students from the Centre: Julian Evans, Jessica Ellis, and Sangie Zaitsoff. We would like to thank Professor Helen Fielding for her generosity in making this interview possible as well as Dr. Ortega for her time and intellect.

‡ ‡ ‡

Julian: You describe your book *In-Between* as a "hometactic" that tries to find a sense of belonging in the discipline of philosophy. You suggest at the outset that philosophy has often sought general and abstract explanations for selfhood and identity, whereas your work aims to investigate the particular embodied experience of those at the margins: people of colour, immigrants and border-dwellers, for example. How does the *mestiza* theory that you present in your book, particularly your concepts of multiplicitous selfhood and being-between-worlds, challenge our fundamental understanding of what philosophy is?

Mariana Ortega: I think that is an interesting way of asking the question. I do think that the mestiza theory of multiplicitous selves that I introduce does present a challenge, although the question presupposes that there is one understanding of philosophy. I want to be careful because I think that traditionally a lot of philosophers and philosophical schools have tried to present general accounts of selfhood. But of course, various theories have called for that generality differently, so I want to be mindful of that. As to how the account of multiplicitous subjectivity challenges the appeal to generality, it does so in terms of an appeal to the multiplicity of lived experience. I think that the push for generality has led us to abstract selves. The moment that you abstract lived experience, it seems to me that you are literally subtracting all of these moments of embodied experience that are multiple. We live, as I put it, in various worlds. To call for an understanding of the way in which the self is multiplicitous is really to call for a mindfulness of the multiplicity that we live every day as we transverse worlds. So in that sense it is a challenge, especially for the views that are too focused on the transcendental unity of the self. Those accounts are being put to question via this position that calls for an understanding of multiplicity in lived experience.

Julian: What has been the response from the tradition of academic philosophy to your work or to the work of others engaged in similar projects?

MO: Within the tradition of Latina feminism, including Gloria Anzaldúa and María Lugones, multiplicity is an important notion and has been taken up explicitly. However, this is a tradition that has not been studied in academic philosophy. This has to do in part with disciplinarity. Sadly, in most philosophical circles this tradition is not even acknowledged. When it is considered, those who have a more traditional understanding of accounts of self that require a generality understand what Latina feminist views of self are doing as sociological accounts or narratives, or "self-help manifestos." I have heard some students—young philosophy students—describe these views in this way. You read them for your personal benefit, to understand yourself, but philosophically they are not considered meaningful. That is a very standard response, which is actually a response to views such as Fanon's by people who just don't understand the philosophical implications of Fanon's views on embodiment and on Blackness. So I would say that if it's not an erasure, it's a questioning of its philosophical import.

Julian: Your work takes these, as you said, forgotten voices or forgotten theories, but it doesn't just present them and leave them at the margins, it brings them to center stage and questions the tradition at the foundation. I can see the connection to Fanon, because you are asking the same questions that challenge the fundamentals of what philosophy is, and that is exciting to see. It brings up that this work needs to be considered philosophically and not just as a study of identity or as narrative, as you put it.

MO: It's an invitation to philosophers, in a way. I am a pluralist and believe that there are different ways of doing philosophy. I understand why there might be a need to concentrate on linguistic issues depending on the philosophical questions asked. In terms of issues of selfhood, it is important to open up the terrain to include work that has not been traditionally considered philosophical but that indeed has philosophical insights. The task is not only giving an account of self to be included in all the other accounts of selfhood, but it is also an invitation to approach philosophy in a more open and interdisciplinary way. In this sense it is non-normative. Before *In-Between* came out I was talking to someone and I said that it is a Frankenstein book made up of different body parts or ideas from different traditions and I did not know if there would be interest in it. Some people will think that these parts don't go together and maybe they'll think it's horrific and dangerous. Though I use Heidegger, I don't want to centre Heidegger—that is not my aim. Some people misread the book and like it because it's Heideggarian, but the aim was not to centre Heidegger and tack on Gloria Anzaldúa and María Lugones and Linda Martín Alcoff. Rather, it is to show how you can work on the issue of selfhood by way of looking at various traditions and figuring out how these traditions can talk to one another, inform one another, perhaps learn from one another. That was my aim, which opens up the philosophical methodology. The book itself is in-between and it discusses an in-between theory about selves that are in-between.

Jessica: The way that you speak about multiplicity opens up so many questions regarding language and the expression of language, given the different worldings and border crossings, as well as sharing spaces and language. If philosophical language is often prefaced on binaries and concepts that only speak to individualistic existence, which your work is leaving behind, how do we write the new *mestiza*? How do we express language that is a multiplicity, given that language hitherto has been communicated through a singular self? How do we make sense of the singular self and the multiplicity of language?

MO: Your question is an important one regarding the difficulty that arises when naming a particular identity. As Anzaldúa names the "new *mestiza*," she also reifies this subject, both constraining her to specific characteristics attributed to that subjectivity and expanding her so as to include her in a collectivity. As such, naming narrows and sediments the self while, at the same time, provides relational and political possibilities. There is the need for an account that questions traditional dichotomies (i.e. subject/object, inside/outside, self/other) such that to be a self —and this is a connection with traditional phenomenology—is to be a complex self in the making intertwined with the world(s) and other selves. To be you is to be engaged in your various worlds in multiple ways. Yet, if you have a language that says "this is the new *mestiza*," the issue of identity becomes "this is all that I am, this one thing with fixed characteristics." So there is the need for two movements: questioning the dichotomies through which we understand the world itself and at the same time questioning my being a self that can be understood only as one. In the text I really follow Anzaldúa on this. Some people think, "Oh how contradictory to say that the self is one and many, that is ridiculous." Yet Anzaldúa is aware of the problem you raise—of the constraints of language when describing the complexity and multiplicity of the self and lived experience. She's using language, but in the mere naming, using that language to put herself on the map, she's narrowing the possibilities. So what she also has to do is methodologically use different kinds of languages. Spanish here, poetry on one side, more poetic narrative on another, and much more theoretical language in different texts, such as in some sections of *Luz en lo Oscuro*. If you read *Luz en lo Oscuro*, it's almost as if her poetic side got diminished. It's much more academic, she is being more of a student. I think language can be made multiple by the way we use it in the work, in the text. With our own bodies too, because we talk by using our hands. So if you think of language as expansive, not just in terms of words but in terms of gestures, sounds, you can disperse it so as to capture that multiplicity and not get caught on that oneness that can easily come out the moment you start writing and putting something down on the page. Thus you raise a difficult and important issue that we constantly have to confront. The hard part, I think—this I am getting from Anzaldúa—is that we are a bit seduced by the oneness; we want it, but our lived experience also includes multiplicity in various ways. That is what's seductive and scary about that particular problem.

Sangie: In your discussion of Anzaldúa and Lugones in *In-Between*, you acknowledge that they are guiding you but you are also questioning and challenging them. Do you conceive of trust as having a role in the dynamic between the guide and the guided, in particular regarding plural and contradictory dynamics that may develop from relationships that we have with our mentors, our guides, and ourselves?

MO: That is an extremely important issue for me. I am deeply mistrustful of philosophers and thinkers in general who do not embody or practice their theoretical commitments. I don't believe in purity, having read Anzaldúa and Lugones who really lead us to challenge the idea of purity that a great deal of traditional philosophy embraces. It is deeply problematic to have a commitment to a particular vision of the world, a particular way of being associated with your theory, and not to embody it or practice it. It has to do with trust. It is difficult to see thinkers completely negating their views, their actions countering what they claim. While it is not possible always to embody our theories, it is still important to try to do so. Trust is diminished if we continue to theorize about the need for coalitional and decolonial practices while at the same time engaging in anti-coalitional and colonialist practices. So I do think that there is an element of trust in relation to a guide, the way you are putting it, or to a mentor, or to someone who inspires you. With writers who are no longer around, I don't know how to approach it. To me it is more of an intuition from the text, given the way they present themselves, whether trust is open. Given your question about language, Jessica, there is maybe something about how they use language that allows you to come into their text, in a way that is inviting and generative. There are two levels here: the level of the praxis, but interestingly enough I think trust can be generated at the level of the expression of the text, and it depends on the kind of language you use, what you assume about your reader, how you treat your reader, how you invite your reader. Now that I am starting a new book, that is one question that I have: how do I want to approach the reader? How do I become respectful of the reader? How do I challenge but at the same time invite her? I think the language itself, maybe, reveals whether there can be more or less trust. But at the level of praxis, it is a matter of theorists critically engaging their own views in an embodied manner and of readers expecting that we at least try to "practice what we preach."

Julian: Speaking of writers whose lives don't necessarily match up with their works, I wanted to ask you a bit more about Heidegger. I feel like the book does an excellent job of really deeply exploring how the Latina feminist conceptions of selfhood do relate to Heidegger's work in a very interesting way. But I was left wondering why Heidegger resonated so well with these other thinkers, rather than philosophers such as Deleuze, Foucault or maybe Derrida who also think about multiplicity, embodiment, or radical difference? Why was Heidegger such a key point for this text?

MO: I appreciate your way of asking this important question, as some people ask me in an already accusatory manner, "Why did you use a Nazi?" I just have to be sincere about this: I picked up *Being and Time* and literally from the get go I had the sense that the book had so much to tell me. I fell in love with the text, with the idea that I could get a glimpse into the meaning of being, because I had been thinking about it in terms of life and lived experience. I had a huge rupture in my life. I started reading philosophy in high school and I fell in love with Camus's, *The Myth of Sisyphus*, and at the same time with Plato, *The Republic*, for very different reasons. I had been thinking a lot about what it could mean to be, given that life can be over so quickly that the whole floor can be taken from you. I think when I moved to the US, I never stopped thinking about that question, because I came to the US due to a revolution in Nicaragua, my country of origin. I majored in philosophy in college, and wrote a thesis on Camus. I was obsessed with the question of existence, and *Being and Time* was an invitation to continue thinking about the elusiveness of being, and I really got caught up in the systematic thinking of it.

I do think that there are better thinkers that I could have used and could have added to the text; to be frank, it did not have to be Heidegger. Politically, it definitely should not have been Heidegger. In fact, that is one of the reasons why I stopped writing the book and did not think that I was going to continue it. At one point I felt that it would be embarrassing to write a text where I continue to make the connection that I had made years ago in a *Hypatia* article ("New *Mestizas*, World-Travelers, and Dasein: Phenomenology and the Multi-Voiced, Multi-Cultural Self"). Someone asked me, "Why did you continue to use Heidegger after that article? You should have dropped him." I have to agree that there is some good reason for believing that I should have dropped him. Yet, I have good reasons as to why I did not. I find Heidegger's description of the self as really capturing key aspects of experience. But what struck me is that even though this account is so generative and is attuned to lived experience, it did not match with the accounts of lived experience I was reading in Black and Latina feminist texts. There were numerous questions that I wanted to keep thinking about at the intersection of these texts. There are certainly difficult questions regarding my choice to work with phenomenology, specifically Heideggerian phenomenology. I refuse to be told what I can and cannot think together—what precludes openings that I might want to explore. This is not to say that I do not care about the political question in Heidegger. It was a difficult project precisely because doubts about my appeal to his work continued as I kept writing, and thus I opted to engage metaphysical questions while at the same time recognizing the difficult questions that remained. I held on to what I think was an opening to re-think, to re-orient traditional phenomenology, and specifically his work, in fruitful ways.

Jessica: Anzaldúa's later version of selfhood, *la nepantlera*, is a self that does not form self-understandings based on race, sex, gender, and other forms of what she describes as external forms of identification. At several points you refer to this approach as intersectional, as well as intermeshed, or intermeshedness, and you use those terms interchangeably. Do you think that it is at all problematic to use the word intersectional, given the baggage that it has within some feminist trends or with some feminist thinkers who criticize it because intersectionality is based on external categories of sex, gender, and race intersecting? Some have argued that it is too smooth of an analysis, because it doesn't explain the conditions that gave rise to those categories in the first place. I am thinking of social reproduction Marxist feminist theorists who are in the business right now of criticizing intersectionality and I am wondering, when you use that word in your book, are you thinking of it in a different way? I like the term intermeshedness, I think it grabs more of what's going on. When I read intersectional, I have these feminists in my head saying, "We're criticizing that term because it relies on external categories," even though you're arguing that Anzaldúa is trying to get outside of categories and external forms of identification.

MO: I want to clarify that María Lugones also has a critique, interestingly enough, of intersectionality. She changes from using intersectionality to intermeshedness. Jennifer Nash has a very well-known article on intersectionality ["Re-thinking Intersectionality"] in which she provides a critique of the theory of intersectionality. There are also three new texts on intersectionality that are dealing with all of these issues. The more standard criticism is that when you look at the intersectional approach, and you have all of these different categories intersecting, the issue is not that they are categories—they can be seen as oppressions, for example—the issue is that you can think of each one separately, and then put them together and get an intersection. You work at the intersection, but you are saying that it is possible look at race, gender, etc. separately.

I read Kimberlé Crenshaw and Patricia Hill Collins as recognizing different issues and problems with the notion of intersectionality throughout their numerous writings. We must be careful not to homogenize or simplify the various intersectional accounts. While some early accounts may be read as less attuned to the problem of the possibility of the separability of the accounts or not providing enough discussion regarding the reasons for the oppression, I think that they still capture important insights about the lived condition of women of color. This is the reason why I continue to use the notion of intersectionality and connect it to Lugones's idea of intermeshedness. In my view these two notions are not opposed to one another, as I recognize the intertwining of the categories even in the early writings on intersectionality. I think that it is still a very good heuristic device, as Hill Collins reminds us. Unfortunately, the debate about intersectionality has become very theoretical and many times misses the original and what I think is the crucial aspect of the notion, bringing to light the material, lived experience of women of color in the contexts of various erasures, oppressions, and violence. One of the current criticisms is that it has been taken away from the context of the law, for which it was originally intended. Nevertheless, as Kathryn Gines has discussed, even before Crenshaw applied the notion within the legal context, various Black thinkers were already working within an intersectional framework. Various Latinas were also writing from a point of view informed by the interaction of multiple oppressions. I still find the notion of intersectionality as incredibly helpful and important in the context of the lives of women of color.

Sangie: In your article "Being Lovingly, Knowingly Ignorant," you challenge and extend Marilyn Frye's account of loving perception and develop an account of loving, knowing ignorance. In "Altars for the Living," you ask what an aesthetics of ignorance might look like. I am wondering if you could speak to the relation between loving, knowing ignorance and an aesthetics of ignorance - is there a way in which you're thinking of them together?

MO: There is definitely a connection. In "Being Lovingly, Knowingly Ignorant," I loved trying to capture contradictory feelings that I have, contradictory positions. For example, how you can love women of colour, study them, and at the same time be clueless about what you are doing and how your actions may actually do violence to their work, to their being. I know that the idea of home is a myth, but I also want it. So I am trying to capture these difficult moments—I am very interested in writing about themes that are hard to write about, for example, moments of contradictions.

My new project is about trying to see how ignorance can be created by way of the aesthetic. I plan to think about how we have used art, maybe in projects that we think are promoting goodness and justice, but at the same time might be reifying other problematic issues. Because I am fascinated by the relationship between image and word, I want to see how we have done with art what we have done with feminism, with theoretical feminism, or what white feminism has done by thinking, "I am helping here, I want to read more about women of colour." Think of the statement, "I am going to give women of colour a voice," or, "I am going to represent people of colour." What if you represent them in ways that are inappropriate, hurtful, or wrong, especially if you have the point of view of someone from a dominant identity? Even if I am a Latina representing Latinas, how do I promote ignorance by way of perception and artistic engagement? On the other side, I want to show how the aesthetic can open up some doors to understand people who have been made invisible or who have been misunderstood; the "Altars for the Living" piece is a part of that project, as it engages the possibility of making visible a group of people who have become invisible (as well as hypervisible in some contexts)—border-crossers escaping poverty and violence in their countries.

Sangie: In the "Being Lovingly, Knowingly Ignorant" paper, you mention that the project is archaeological—are you thinking of this new work in that way, as an uncovering? There's a sense in which there is love there, in the project of making visible or even reorienting, in the sense of Sara Ahmed's work…

MO: Think of it in terms of multiple ways, multiple sightings of love, in a sense. There's the love that the artist or the feminist or the white feminist has that moves them to create work or to create a theory that encompasses women of colour, and there's the love—my love—in uncovering how we have been hurt, in uncovering how other women of colour have already told us that this is happening and they have not been heard. So I am curious, concentrating on photography, how it has happened in photography. I want to see how photography was used supposedly lovingly, but did not work.

Julian: In "Altars for the Living," you engage the deep, tragic, and horrific violence that is taking place every day at the US-Mexico border, but the words and the images that you used during your talk and the photos that you chose really opened up a space for the audience to connect emotionally and effectively with what you were talking about. Most photographs close us off because it is so horrific, so violent and gruesome. Perhaps you could tell us more about how that project is taking shape and where it is going next, how you are using images or photos in a way that haunts us and allows us to emotionally and effectively get a sense of this violence that we are often told to think about but don't actually connect with.

MO: Well, I love art. I love poetry. Words don't fail for me when I read poetry that I love, but it seems to me that calling for empathy or feeling with others' pain doesn't seem to be working in terms of theoretical approaches. This is the reason why I am studying aesthetics and thinking seriously about images, especially photographic representation. I am trying to figure out if there are ways in which I can use images to disclose and uncover moments of violence that people don't want to see but are there and have become transparent and part of the everyday. In "Altars for the Living," I am using the work of a particular photographer, Verónica Gabriela Cárdenas. In another work I am using photographs of objects left behind by those who perished in the desert while crossing the US-Mexico border. I have been moved by the way the audience has reacted to my discussion of those photographs in the context of a discussion of bodies of color as bodies of sorrow. The photographs represent not mere objects but dreams lost, lives interrupted in their pursuit of the so-called American dream. Like *In-Between*, the new project will gather together material from various traditions in philosophy and various disciplines: photographic history and theory, epistemology of ignorance, Latina art criticism, and photographic representations of *Latinidad*. I am making a connection there with the idea that bodies of colour are bodies of sorrow. It is going to be a very different kind of book because I am mixing photography that is artistic but also photography of common objects with photographic history, philosophy of photography, philosophy of art and epistemology in terms of epistemology of ignorance.

Julian: This new work is forcefully critical of the border. Given the political climate in the US right now, this is challenging work, and it must take a lot of hope and courage to be a Latina feminist at this moment. How do you find the possibilities of carrying on this work, given that the political situation looks so bleak right now?

MO: This semester I have been reading outside of philosophy. I've read some books on sociology, a little bit of anthropology, and geography on borders and borderlands, in particular the US and Mexico border. I also took a look at some poetry books inspired by border crossing. It is very hard because it makes me both furious and incredibly sad. I was a refugee, but I had the luck of not having to cross that border. I cannot imagine how people make it. So many don't, and if they do they have been raped, they have been treated so horribly. After college I was an English as a Second Language Teacher and worked with students who had these experiences. It is so heart-wrenching to see how Latinxs and Latin Americans are being described in the media, as if they are only, we are only, criminals. There is currently tremendous racism and animosity against Latinxs and Latin Americans on the part of the U.S administration and a great part of the population. I recently read an article discussing the way in which there have been incidents of racism in Wal-Marts, where people explicitly voice their racist views to perceived Latinx/Latin American as well as Muslim customers. Incidents of explicit racism and hate are increasing. This is especially difficult to witness as Latinxs/Latin Americans work incredibly hard to contribute to the US economy. It is important to do this kind of work precisely because of this climate. I suppose that I still have some hope, perhaps "anxious hope" as I believe we need to continue to write, to think, to explore these issues even when it is depressing and difficult, even when reading itself creates discomfort. I taught a freshman seminar years ago on the Rwandan genocide, and one of the books was absolutely horrifying. I remember taking a class on the Holocaust in college…you keep reading it, and why? Because you know that you *have* to know this. You cannot *not* know this. Yet, it is not just about knowing. Hopefully, you will feel something as well, because there is another problem: even when there is knowledge about the pain and injustices of others, especially selves at the margins, people living in poverty, racialized bodies, LGBTQ selves, immigrants, refugees—those that Anzaldúa calls *los atravesados*—there is lack of feeling, empathy, and action. It goes well beyond knowledge.

Thank you Julian, Jessica, and Sangie for your interest in my travels to the in-between and for our conversation.

THE RELATIONSHIP OF TEMPORALITY IN AUTOBIOGRAPHY TO TRANS-NARRATIVE FORM

JESSICA ELLIS

In his latest work on transsexual narratives (trans-narratives) and autobiographies, Jay Prosser observes the unavoidable split that occurs within the subject through the process of being one who is both at the same time enunciating and being enunciated about. The self-reporting subject must come to grapple with being a narrator of their first person experience as well as organize these thoughts as part of a detached, objective third person point of view that is spoken to another. To narrate as part of these two perspectives creates a split and contradictory subject position that undermines a trans person's claims to identity in the present. This is because transsexual subjectivity is expected to inhabit either a before or after transition position, never an open-ended prospect. Yet, communicating these narratives is necessary as "autobiography is transsexuality's proffered symptom," and the presence of gender dysphoria is not locatable biologically.[1] As the recounting of personal stories are heavily relied upon for diagnosis as well as access to hormone therapies and surgeries, their interpretation has grave consequences for some trans people who are often pressured into lying or manipulating accounts of their past to fit existing acceptable narrative schemas.

Prosser maintains that autobiographies, or "body narratives" (trans-narratives) help produce a representation of embod-

1 Jay Prosser, *Second Skins* (New York: Columbia University Press, 1998), 104.

ied transsexual subjectivity through the interplay of body and narrative. One important aim of this method is to show that the material world and flesh that it supports have an impact on the way theory presents gender. This approach is largely in response to his criticism that gender studies inaugurated gender constitution as socially constructed and thus disembodied. Prosser also seeks to draw attention to the relationship between the psyche and gender identity, which is lacking in analyses that focus on how institutions reinforce gender norms.[2] The framing of narratives into autobiographical form, Prosser argues, joins the past and present within the trans person's psyche to form a coherent subject position and thus heals the split.[3] By placing the onus on the way the narrative is framed to establish trans subjectivity, and by advancing what I argue is a somewhat narrow analysis of narrative temporality, Prosser seems to elide the relationship between how the body and subjectivity write and conduct each other. His prescient analysis, though politically and incredibly necessary for enriching the theory canon, could perhaps become an even stronger account with an expanded look at how the material world influences narrative form. This would make trans-narratives more embodied accounts because subjectivity becomes tied to materiality.

To tie materiality to narrative form one must consider that story genres like autobiography are imbued with literary elements that speak to dominant epistemes of the time said genre emerged. Different types of stories render or express temporality in different ways depending on the social situation of the time period that gave rise to such ideas. Thus language expresses more than just words and narrative form is more than an empty container to fill—it contains a history that influenced its making and also continues to influence an individual's thought. Autobiographical time, for Prosser, focuses instead on merely the form of narrative itself, not how narrative is influenced by the socio-historical context of its

2 Prosser's criticisms of gender theory can be found in *Assuming a Body: Transgender and Rhetorics of Materiality* by Gayle Salamon, specifically pp. 38-41.

3 Ibid., 123.

making; the history of how the form emerged is fetishized and overpowered by the resultant external structure. As a response to this concern, this paper will outline a more embodied theory of the relationship between autobiographical time, subjectivity and language by taking into account Bakhtin's material theory of time and space in the concept of the "chronotope."

I. Trans-narratives and Autobiography

Trans autobiographies produce an inherent tension between two psyches. Firstly, a consciousness that has always historically been, is then suddenly replaced via the act of retroactivity by another who has presumably also always existed. The "moment" where the psyche splits between these two identities is assumed to be that pivotal rift where the trajectory of the transsexual aligns with a transitional experience in the narrative. For example, when Jan Morris looks at herself in the mirror to say goodbye to her old self, this is where she also becomes her new self through the decision to have sexual reassignment surgery (SRS)[4]. The creation of this "split" literary consciousness can become problematic for transsexuals telling their story who do not have a such a clear Joycean epiphany. This approach perhaps may also alienate transgender people who do not seek to fully become the other gender—do not have a definite split—but perhaps still wish to learn about and explore medicalized options with support. The split consciousness advanced by Prosser begets an expectation that not every trans person can match. His work in *Second Skins* focuses specifically on transsexuals not multiple types of transgender identities, but I argue his ideas are still productive on the whole when considering other trans subjectivities possibly caught up in the idea that they are inhabiting some sort of contested or split consciousness.

In order to make Prosser's body trans-narratives more productive for not just transsexual narrative theory but also for understanding other types of transgender narratives, the limitations of a split consciousness should be questioned. I maintain that the

---

4 Ibid., 99.

idea of a split is theoretically too smooth for understanding trans subjectivity because it lends itself to a stultifying conception of time. It cannot account for trans folk who have more complicated ideas surrounding their own identity that cannot fit into the before and after framing. Prosser's work focuses on the transsexual caught between the past and present identity marked by a desire to be another sex, but it is important not to forget about other trans identities who may be at various stages of transition or do not wish to fully transition at all. It is also important to note that the word desire is lacking for there is also a sense of deep embodied realization manifesting in the psyche that one does not desire to be, but already *is* the other sex. Yet, Gordon Olga Mackenzie raises an important concern: "If it were not for [especially binary] gender oppression, transsexuals would not be likely to seek SRS."[5] This concern, however, must still be reconciled with members of trans communities who would still seek SRS due to a felt sense of gender. It is of especial necessity, moreover, to make sure that narrative temporalities do not minimize the potential for ever-evolving consciousness that may be felt or experienced by trans folk regardless of if they identify with a specific gender or not.

The Gender Movement challenges the assimilation of gender minority groups into the dominant culture, which insists upon contiguity between anatomy and lived gender.[6] Such groups should have the same access to services even if their stories do not fit a typical trans-narrative schema. Robert, a trans man explains that such "hallway" dwellers do not wish to be one sex or the other and are quite comfortable in the state of "in-betweenness." Though many trans folk, including Prosser, do indeed identify with one gender, the institutionalized pressure to conform to a single gender may have the undesirable result of delegitimizing alternative gender orientations that ought to exist as viable subjectivities that engage with and perceive the world:

---

5 Patricia Elliot and Katrina Roen, "Transgenderism and the Question of Embodiment," *GLQ: A Journal of Lesbian and Gay Studies* 4, no. 2 (1998): 240

6 Ibid.

> These doors open and shut but at the end of the day you can only open a door into the male world on one side and the female world on the other side and you've joined society on either side. But if you stay in the hallway, which I believe is much more freeing because you're not bound by either side, it's infinitely harder because you're not bound by either side and you're not belonging to either side. The hallway I think is a wonderful place. Hallways can have windows and they can have wonderful views.[7]

These "hallway" subjectivities are not realized in Prosser's trans-narratives because they are not "split" between a past and a present identity—their very identity sits comfortably in transit. The limited scope of trans-narratives becomes problematic because it also leaves out the ability to make reference to other possible transgender identities.[8] Trans-narratives are only amenable to transsexuals who see a before and after. Opening up the boundaries of trans-narratives to make space for other trans identities does not require a loss of the specificities of transsexual subjectivity; there is a unique transsexual experience Prosser offers us that cannot be lost. I merely contest that the account of embodiment in general within trans-narratives can become more robust if the idea of a "split" in subjectivity and temporality is questioned. And if this past/present temporality that gives rise to the split is weakened, this can make space for looking at other trans identities. Further it can help us think better in terms of how their autobiographies can be communicated in a theoretically strong way that maintains the integrity and accuracy of trans experience without it being oppressed by harmful literary elements.

The limitations of reading the typical "split" become clear, once the multitude of gender identities other than transsexuality emerge. Given the multiple identity alignments at stake, personal narratives should illuminate the multiplicity of possible identity trajectories that include staying somewhere in-between. This acceptance, however, can only be realized if the medical community

7 Sara Davidmann, "Border Trouble: photography, strategies and transsexual identities," *Scan* 3, no. 3 (2006).

8 Ibid.

gives up the desire to treat trans folk as guilty until proven innocent. Trans folk are the only group forced to prove their identity, and this pressure no doubt obfuscates their ability to communicate an accurate autobiography. As Judith Butler and others argue, this pressure manifests through the power of the medical gaze on the trans object, which must conform to fit the appropriate role to gain legitimacy. This disciplinary mechanism is at work during self-reporting practices.[9] The medical field, argues Butler, needs to take into account desires for stable identity that are crucial to realize a livable life that requires various degrees of stability.[10] Yet, there is a double-standard for what the definition of stability requires for trans folk. It is acceptable for cisgender people to go through phases, make bad choices, have doubts and experiment with self-identity, but trans folk's choices are more rigidly interrogated simply on the basis of the fact that they were born into a sexed body that does not represent their felt gendered identity. I take it to be a systemic form of discrimination to treat trans folk differently and to institutionalize differing expectations of such individuals within the medical community simply based on how they wish to present themselves to the world. The root of this discrimination rests in the fact that gender dysphoria is the only condition in The Diagnostic and Statistical Manual of Mental Disorders (DSM) that is dealt with not by finding a cure, but by working retroactively through it by proving it exists in the first place.[11] Yet, there is a myriad of problems with treating something that is not a disease, within the same epistemological framework that works to treat illness; People that are not broke, do not need fixing. Those without mental disorder diagnoses in the DSM are permitted to change behaviour inside and outside the medical system based on how they feel, but this privilege is not extended to trans folk even though they are technically also outside of the realm of mental disorder. Cosmetic surgery is of especial importance here when aesthetic restructuring results in a double-standard. If gender dysphoria is outside

9 Judith Butler, *Undoing Gender* (New York: Routledge, 2004), 67.
10 Ibid., 8.
11 Prosser, *Second Skins*, 107.

the scope of mental illness then responses to desires for aesthetic restructuring should be handled in a similar manner for both trans and cis-gender people.

II. Limitations of the Relationship Between Temporality and Embodiment in Trans-narratives

The clinical episodic narrative follows a linear progression that has a particular *telos* in mind at its outset—a voyage with a destination. Symbols and language reminiscent of travel and finding oneself on this journey are punctuated by accepted key moments of realization like the boy who is caught wearing his mom's shoes and the girl who rejects Barbie Dolls. Prosser notes, "the 'odyssey' is as much the writing as the life, for it is the writing that allows this scripted navigation into life."[12] In this autobiographical framework, the trans-narrator is aware of the end of the story, as it is still being lived. Prosser notices that this progression is not unidirectional, however, in that autobiography involves a "temporal double movement" in which the narrator reaches back into the past to propel this past through the present.[13] This double movement is carefully illustrated through a vivid recounting of the see-saw personality of Dick and Renée. The past identity of Dick comes into conflict with and also at times attempts to write over the present identity of his female alter-ego Renée during a sexual encounter with a club owner who wants to see her as a gay man and not the transgender woman she is. Prosser argues that framing narrative through this temporal double movement thus has the ability to make embodied transsexual subjectivity possible in that it allows the transsexual to integrate the self, from within the body, after transition. The sex change was a deeply signifying moment for Renée, so much that even when past feelings of Dick tried to overwrite her subjectivity, she still *felt* she was now a woman.[14] The split "body narrative" explains her emotions and lived experience now as a woman; Prosser

12 Ibid., 116.
13 Ibid., 117.
14 Ibid., 123.

believes this is how body and narrative construct each other and compose transsexual subjectivity.

The example of Dick and Renée works well to illustrate the body narrative in action, but my contention with Prosser's explanation is that it does not explain how self-awareness of one's subjectivity or consciousness is produced by the body's experience within the narrative. It explains how Jan Morris and Renée can trace their feelings as women back to a moment of self-acceptance that then changed the trajectory of their lives. His interpretation of time structured by the autobiographical return supposedly also structures the narrator's subjectivity, but he evades any real discussion of subjectivity proper other than to comment regarding the moment where the split is healed, and transsexual identity is made possible. Yet, the autobiographical framework is much more complex in its relation to the structuring of the consciousness that it frames. For Biddy Martin, bodies and psyches are never purely effects of discursive [or narratological] practices or of abstract power relations; invested with the historicity of lived experience, they also have the potential to "exert pressure" on the normalizing processes through which they are constructed.[15] This line of thought presumes there is a material aspect to the development of subjectivity. It is not clear, however, in Prosser's work how the transsexual narrator is able to exert pressure on the world through the body and vice versa, especially given what he takes to be a position of embodied subjectivity. The body's influence on subjectivity is overdetermined by the narrative structure in which it is framed, thus abstracting conscious production from the material realm. A productive material explanation to find the connection between how one's subjectivity actually changes from being a body in the world, is Karl Marx's materialist conception of history. This theory contends that it is through one's actions or labour, from within a body situated in history and subject to historical contingencies, that consciousness changes. Marx maintains, "While man works on nature and changes it, he simultaneously changes his own na-

15 Patricia Elliot and Katrina Roen, "Transgenderism and the Question of Embodiment," 236.

ture. He develops the potencies slumbering in it, and subjects the play of its powers to his own sway."[16] Human labour or activity is the conscious exercise of our power over nature, and through this embodied position, we are affected by nature, just as much as we affect it ourselves.

III. Reading Trans-narratives through the Chronotope

The contributions of literary theorist Mikhail Bakhtin augment the forgoing Marxist arguments because his work focuses not just on the material world and consciousness, but how the connection between these two makes its way into expressions of thought such as language and literature. More specifically, he offers literary theory and philosophy a richer view of the connection between the material world, and time-space in various literary genres within which he worked. For him, time and space are not two distinct realms that can be studied in isolation. The chronotope marks the inseparability of time and space as it refers to "the intrinsic connectedness of temporal and spatial relationships that are artistically expressed in literature." Bakhtin calls this spatio-temporal configuration of the individual within each genre the chronotope (time-space).[17] The chronotope is constitutive of the specific ways time and space are rendered in each genre given the preoccupations of said genre. Each genre distinctively moulds its characters in a way according to the typical emotions, situations, and values of that narrative type. The connection between the specifics of each genre forms the identity of the subject. Thus the different stylings of time and space organize bodies, which create spaces for the development of certain types of literary consciousness. The chronotope gives the reader a way to read not just the events, but the way identity is made by the spatio-material world of the genre. The trans-narrative is conflicted in that it is stuck in a form of the

16 Karl Marx, *Capital: Volume 1*, trans. Ben Fowkes (Toronto: Penguin Books, 1990), 283.

17 Mikhail Bakhtin,"Forms of Time and of the Chronotope in the Novel" in *The Dialogic Imagination*, ed. Michael Holquist. (Austin: UTP, 1981), 85.

past of the epic where such identities are not malleable because the specifics of the form homogenize individual personality/identity, and yet is also reaching toward the dynamism of novel where characters are free to develop in a variety of ways.

It can be said that the problem with autobiography as a means to account for split subjectivity, is that the subject is not only split between two subjectivities, but between two narrative styles or literary genres, the "epic" and the "novel" which influence the construction of the subject in different ways depending on how each genre has organized time and space. The subjectivity of the character of the Epic, for example, is the hero who follows a specific plot trajectory. The character of the novel, however, as a more open-ended representation, is able to interrogate the consciousness-building and breaking of its characters in a dynamic way. The novel's character development is redefined constantly as there is no overdetermined or generic plot for a novel to follow. Trans-narrative subjectivity, I argue, appears to be caught between assuming the role of the hero in the epic—dominated by the authority of the past—and the flexibility and transgressions of a character developing and interrogating its own thoughts within the novel.

The epic represents a character subjectivity that is trapped in the past, whereas the novel's character is bound up in the present state of immediate self-consciousness, a voice reflecting upon the self and events. The epic is detached from all self-conscious experience because the form of the genre takes precedence, it is unchangeable and lacks dynamism. Further, this genre operates from a distance rather than an autobiographical or self-narration perspective; the form affirms an authority of the past over the present. History—"ancestors", "memory","first" and "beginning"—is valued more than one's present. Such valorization renders the epic a closed-off genre or finalized form. In addition, the epic marks the past as sacred and no present character is able to question this authority by enacting a double-voice that questions events as they unfold. The character's feelings (consciousness) has no place in this genre. Bakhtin explains, "In ancient literature it is memory, and not knowledge, that serves as the source and power for the creative impulse."[18] Trans folk are caught in the trappings of the epic's pervasive influence on discourse as the pressure of the past, not the present, becomes the source of knowledge over and above present personal experience. Memory and personal history is interrogated and more value is put on proving their present identity based on the authority of the past to back up these present claims. Temporality in this sense is focused on past events. More than this, the temporality of the epic is the time-space of the world of the patriarchal social structures of "fathers" and is "thus separated from other classes by a distance that is almost epic."[19] The authority of the medical system to insist on the past as truth is one example why expanding analysis of narrative temporality is an important step towards smashing the hegemony of the patriarchy.

Bakhtin analyzes multiple types of novels and they all share a defining trait that continuously comes into conflict with the epic. The defining trait of the genre is that it forsakes the past as the source of knowledge and shifts emphasis back to the present. Bakhtin argues, "To portray an event on the same time-and-value plane as oneself and one's contemporaries (and an event that is therefore based on personal experience and thought) is to undertake a radical revolution, and to step out of the world of epic into the world of the novel."[20] I believe the novel of "adventure-time" represents the closest style guide to how trans folk report their personal history. This style contains a more linear conception of time and comes into conflict with the demands of the epic whose sole authority is the past. In this form, the sequence of events becomes tied to the progression of the character's journey. Put another way, events are able to change the character's thoughts and feelings as the story progresses. Experience and knowledge become the driving force behind this genre, not the demands of the form such as tradition.

The autobiography as a whole contains a contest between

---

18 Mikhail Bakhtin,"Epic and Novel" in *The Dialogic Imagination*, ed. Michael Holquist. (Austin: UTP, 1981), 15.

19 Ibid.

20 Ibid., 14.

two competing genres and authorities over the individual. The pressure manifests in a lack of authenticity at times where the form of the epic takes over and minimizes the strength of the conviction of the present voice. The result is the pressure for trans folk to have to manipulate their stories to straddle both genres. Memory (epic) is given precedence as identity must be proved through the past, and this account is given more consideration than the trans folk's present account (novel) of the current thoughts and feelings surrounding their identity.

An important aspect to consider when analyzing the novel and narratives is that self-consciousness or the inner voice of the character, did not always exist. The ancient voice represented the state and tradition. It was public, oral and it is only later that the reflective, questioning inner monologue emerged, and then was transposed into literary form. The novel is able to make use of the turn in public to private discourse, yet there is always tension between the two because one's public voice is oriented toward the state and its institutions while the inner private voice is able to question and find their own truth. The novel voice is politically important because it gives a voice to question and potentially change the form. It gives the authority back to the character, which is important as trans people should have authority over their own narratives because they are the main character in their autobiography. That is to say that the emphasis in medical contexts should not be on trans people to prove their identity through the authority of the past, but to shift the value of narrative towards the present. Following from these observations, it becomes clear that there is not simply a doubling of time, as Prosser argues, but that time figures individuals differently within its scope depending on how the story is organized by the teller. The temporality of "split" consciousness that the transsexual experiences is perhaps a split that can be healed less by looking at not just narrative form, but by looking at the ways narrative form influences the authorship of self-expression.

IV. Conclusion

My hopes in drawing attention to the way narrative is framed and influenced by the chronotope is to show that the Epic mirrors the clinical gaze. The gaze and the drive for the trans person to become an authority of their own produces issues that could be remedied through more careful attention to what influences narrative style. The distance of the sterilized medicalized interpretation conflicts with and gravitates away from elements of the novel, which can account more for variegated interpretations of conscious development (think of the hyper-developed consciousness of the characters in classic novels like Fyodor Dostoevsky's *The Brothers Karamazov*). Hilary Malatino argues that trans-narratives [that mimic the epic and clinical gaze] may fall victim to the problems of the guest lecture in that they remain ignorant to epistemological concerns.[21] It should be noted here that by trans-narratives she does not mean specifically Prosser's trans-narratives but a broader sense of self-reporting by various trans individuals. She explains:

> I stay away from conventional (that is, triumphal) coming-out narratives that conclude with individualized banalities about the importance of being true to one's self and finding self-fulfillment, happiness, or some other dangling existential carrot. Instead, I utilize texts in which the autobiographical elements are interwoven with meditations on phenomena like institutional exclusion, the trouble with the medicalization of gender, the experience of being marked for social death, or the technoscientific developments that have shaped the contemporary terrain of gender transition.[22]

Malatino seems to be describing ethnographical writings here, but the problem with these is perhaps that trans folk unaware of the influence of discourse on self-reporting would have no way of knowing that they ought to weave their story through such a critical framework. The coming-out tropes are reproduced because they

---

21 Hilary Malatino, "Pedagogies of Becoming," *TSQ Transgender Studies Quarterly* 2, no. 3 (2015): 398.

22 Ibid.

are accepted and to question them, is to potentially lose access to therapy and/or treatment. While I agree with Malatino that traditional narratives are fraught with problematic elements, we should focus on why this is, and try to question narrative authority itself.

Another limitation of the ethnological approach is that it does not look deeply into how class affects linguistic choice or what is really behind the words people use. As hermeneutical tools, sociological methods such as ethnography are quite limited. Moreover, there is problem with assuming that ethnography and not literary theory can comprehend the value of what Bahktin calls "speech-genres." His theory of such genres sets in motion, "the internal stratification of any single national language into social dialects, characteristic group behaviour, professional jargons, generic languages, languages of generations and age groups, tendentious languages, languages of the authorities, of various circles and of passing fashions, languages that serve the specific socio-political purposes of the day."[23] Speech-genres thus represent the socio-cultural aspects of the chronotope and illuminate the way the specificities of language are worked reciprocally through narrative and the body organized within spatio-temporality. This is an important point to mark as "The separation of style and language from the question of genre has been largely responsible for a situation in which only individual and period-bound overtones of a text are the privileged subjects of study, while its basic social tone is ignored."[24] Prosser arguably focuses more on the overtones of style in his analysis of the autobiographic style, thus re-inscribing elements of the medical gaze associated with the epic. The specific language, inaugurated through the chronotope, communicates the body's spatio-temporal relationship with the social and the consciousnesses of the character is made by and makes the story because of this; the climate of the time each genre was instantiated, manifests itself throughout such respective elements of each genre.

---

23 Mikhail Bakhtin, "Discourse in the Novel," in *The Dialogic Imagination: Four Essays,* ed. Caryl Emerson and Michael Holquist (Texas: University of Texas Press, 1981), 262-3.

24 Ibid., 269

Each narrative style is thus imbued with a social character that is fetishized, by Prosser in this case, by our focus on language as abstracted from the construction of literary subjectivity. To account for embodied subjectivity requires an analysis of language that recognizes the constraints associated with certain narrative tendencies. Speech-genres, and the chronotope to which they belong, account for such tendencies.

Preserving the narrative is important to Prosser, as he argues it can be read in a way that allows a space for trans subjectivity to emerge. His argument is largely a response in resistance to the overvaluation of technology or certain interpretations of performativity as establishing trans subjectivity.[25] His project is fascinating, but the subtext of his argument is problematic in that it assumes subjectivity can have an identity trajectory at the outset, and that this can then be traced through narrative. Even though transsexual subjectivity is certainly split, implementing a before and after temporality limits the narrative analysis. This position may also alienate trans people who do not yet know what their true identity is, and are still writing and want to keep writing their story. The problem is that the form limits the possibility for an open-ended sense of identity because it pre-emptively expects an "after." I think the form should always reflect an openness, especially with trans people who are underexposed to trans culture, or have never met a trans person before, and so do not know how to navigate potential crises of identity and gender dysphoria; children especially run the risk of not understanding their feelings about their identity. Some trans folk only know something is "off," try to figure it out, and this can include crossing, maintaining a variety of sexual orientations—things that can work against them or would have to be omitted if a typical trans-narrative were attempted that relies on a before/after schema. The unedited raw footage of the personal narrative often conflicts with literary tropes and needs to be inherently accepted as possibly chaotic, and full of mistakes. The internalized double-voice of self-conscious narrative opposed to the finalization of the epic, allows for continuous regeneration

25 Prosser, *Second Skins*, 133.

of meaning and becoming.[26]After all, it would be abnormal to assume people are born knowing exactly who they will be. Rather than trying to use narrative to heal a split, splits should be seen as integral to human experience, part of the dynamism of narrative form. Splits and breaks should form the basis for a possibly new trans-narrative form that seeks to push away from elements that are imbued with linear (heterosexual) conceptions of time that foreclose upon fluid conscious experience. The before and after trope is important to stress in trans-narratives because the juxtaposition ends up highlighting the realness of the present gender, the legitimacy of which must be taken seriously. I do not, however, think this stylistic element should form a crucial aspect of any narrative theory seeking to demolish patriarchal thought.

The re-reading of narratives would also speak more to the push for the change in diagnostic language from gender dysphoria to gender dissonance—a state of social and/or mental distress due to navigating one's feelings about their identity. In this way gender is not seen as an individual's internal—and pathological—struggle, but rather part of the greater social context from which gender is reinforced and how this oppresses non-cisgender folk. The idea of dissonance can relate to a disruptive narrative or struggle rather than the traditional narrative that seeks to fit the DSM model. [27] My hopes in this paper have been to not take away from Prosser's critical analysis here, but to simply expand its potential by providing a roust literary critique of narratives in general as a means to bolster and support his work. A narrative form less constrained by the chronotope of the epic could become commensurate with a more open and accepting diagnostic language in medicalizing contexts and contribute to a positive turn in transgender care.

26 Mikhail Bakhtin, "Discourse in the Novel," 324.

27 Kelley Winters, "Gender Dissonance," *Journal of Psychology and Human Sexuality*, no.3-4 (2008) 86.

GENDER IDENTITY TROUBLE

An Analysis of the Underrepresentation of Trans Professors in Canadian Universities*[‡]

ALEXANDRE BARIL, TRANSLATED BY
HÉLÈNE BIGRAS-DUTRISAC AND DAVID GUIGNION

Abstract

This article considers the under-representation of trans persons who specialize in trans issues employed as professors in Canadian universities, with particular attention paid to the case of departments of gender and feminist studies. The research question is: what are the systemic barriers preventing the displacement of the cis-centric subject from the center of francophone Canadian academic feminism, and contributing to the exclusion of trans persons ? This article analyzes these obstacles. The first part demonstrates the presence of cisgenderism in teaching and research, creating a glass ceiling for trans persons in academia. The second studies the absence of trans issues in feminist francophone teaching and research, despite the interest of students in these issues. The third part employs a transfeminist approach to trouble the cisgender normativity of gender and feminist studies and the disciplinary divisions that marginalize trans persons in academia.

‡ We would like to thank Alexandre Baril and *Philosophiques* for allowing us to translate and republish "Trouble dans l'identité de genre : le transféminisme et la subversion de l'identité cisgenre : Une analyse de la sous-représentation des personnes trans* professeur-es dans les universités canadiennes," *Philosophiques*, 44, no. 2, (2017): 285-317.

The data presented in this translation have been updated from the initial publication of this text. All untranslated French language publications referenced in the original publication have been unofficially translated by David Guignion and Hélène Bigras-Dutrisac for the convenience of the reader.

1. Gender Identity Trouble: The Cisgender Subject of Feminism

In 1990, philosopher Judith Butler published *Gender Trouble: Feminism and the Subversion of Identity*. In this book, Butler interrogates the category "woman" that constituted the foundation and basis of feminist movements/studies, with the help of a Foucauldian genealogical method and an "immanent critique,"[1] to detect its mechanisms of exclusion, as well as to identify the novel forms of epistemic violence that produced the identity category of woman as a central concern to the political feminist agenda. Butler notably highlights the heterocentric conditions that have marginalized lesbians from feminism. The title of this article redeploys Butler's title in the spirit of fanfiction, with the addition of an adjective (gender [identity]), which, as asserted by Ann Braithwaite and Catherine M. Orr,[2] remain invisible as much in Butler's title as in other feminist texts, while nonetheless haunting, despite its invisibility, the methodological, epistemological, and political frames of feminist reflections since their conception. In their work, Braithwaite and Orr use simple yet poignant examples of "invisible adjectives" that cut across fields of knowledge and everyday (linguistic) practices, whether speaking of marriage (the invisible adjective being heterosexual, in contrast with the explicitly denoted gay marriage) or of certain professions such as the doctor (the invisible adjective being male, since we must otherwise specify that we are speaking of a female doctor). These "invisible adjectives" denote "unmarked identities,"[3] or those identities of dominant social groups, viewed

1 Judith Butler, *Gender Trouble* (New York: Routledge, 2007), v. ["Immanent critique" is a term usually associated with thinkers of the Frankfurt School of critical theory such as Adorno, and is contrasted with Kant's "transcendental critique." Eds.]

2 Ann Braithwaite and Catherine M. Orr, *Everyday Women's and Gender Studies: Introductory Concept* (New York: Routledge, 2016).

3 Linda R. Waugh, "Marked and Unmarked: A Choice between Unequals in Semiotic Structure," *Semiotica*, 38, no. 3-4 (1982): 299-318.

as natural, universal, and normal, as opposed to marginalized/marked identities, viewed as unnatural, unusual, and abnormal. Such mechanisms of naturalization and normalization of dominant identity categories are foundational to "invisible adjectives." We specify that we are speaking of gay marriage because, in the normalized definition of marriage as heterosexual, an invisible presumption exists, with the paradoxical effect of rendering non-heterosexual unions hyper-visible through a particular lens, while simultaneously rendering them invisible through the normalization of heterosexual unions. Shedding light on these "invisible adjectives," as shown by Braithwaite and Orr, has significant repercussions on our fields of knowledge:

> What becomes apparent in this exercise of uncovering invisible adjectives is that attempts to make any group of previously invisible people visible involve more than just inserting marginalized groups into the universalizing histories of the past. And this realization has led us to think about knowledge differently, about what has counted as knowledge and where and how knowledge could be gleaned. [4]

Though putting such "invisible adjectives" forward constitutes an important task at the heart of anti-oppression studies, including feminist and gender studies, these fields of knowledge are always already marked by concerning absences and erasures in relation to certain dominant categories in which the labour of making unmarked identities visible remains incomplete. In feminist and gender studies, particularly in francophone communities, this is the case for cisgender/cissexual (or cis) identities.[5] It is important

4 Braithwaite and Orr, *Everyday Women's and Gender Studies*, 17.

5 Alexandre Baril, "Transsexualité et privilèges masculins. Fiction ou réalité?," in *Diversité sexuelle et constructions de genre*, ed. Line Chamberland, et al (Québec : Presses de l'Université du Québec, 2009): 263-295. Baril notes that cissexual and cisgender (or cis) people are non-transsexual or non-transgender people. As stated by Baril: "In the field of natural science, the cis adjective is employed as the antonym of trans, the first referring to an element that is on the same side, the second, signifying "beyond" in its Latin origins, referring to an element belonging to both sides. More generally, the trans prefix designates, in contrast to the cis prefix, a transformation and a transition. The cis prefix is

to mention, from the outset, that this occultation of trans* issues through cis norms can be found in all disciplinary fields. The feminist and gender studies case, which is the focus of this article, is therefore just one of many, though it is particularly problematic, since this field of study too often concerns itself with gender issues without addressing the cis presumptions that mark its objects of study. Moreover, although this essay focuses on gender and feminist studies, the implications of the reflections I propose, notably in the concluding section of this article, apply to a wide array of disciplines, including feminist philosophy, by raising ethical and epistemological issues regarding the place of trans* studies in academia.

By paraphrasing Butler's title, the highlighting of "invisible adjectives" allows for the cis-centred character of feminism to become visible, where cis identities are normalized and taken for granted, seen as foundational to feminism and gender. Unless otherwise specified, when feminists refer to gender, they are in no way speaking of gender identity (cis/trans*[6]), but of the masculine/feminine genders, and these are, unless specifically identified as trans*, "naturally" understood as cis. The highlighting of invis-

therefore associated with sex and gender terms to designate those people who decide not to undergo sex or gender transitions."

6 Susan Stryker, *et al*, "Introduction: Trans-, Trans, or Transgender?," *Women's Studies Quarterly*, 36, no. 3-4 (2008): 11-22, http://www.jstor.org.proxy1.lib.uwo.ca/stable/pdf/27649781.pdf. The term trans* with an asterisk is inclusive of different gender identities that exceed binaural sex and gender frames, such as those identifying as transsexual, transgender, non-binary, bigender, agender, two-spirit, transvestite, etc. The expression trans- with a hyphen, as introduced by Stryker, Currah, and Moore, aims to broaden trans- analyses beyond sex and gender issues: "A little hyphen is perhaps too flimsy a thing to carry as much conceptual freight as we intend for it [to] bear, but we think the hyphen matters a great deal precisely because it marks the difference between the implied nominalism of 'trans' and the explicit relationality of 'trans-,' which remains open-ended and resists premature foreclosure by attachment to any single suffix. Our call for papers read: 'Trans, -gender, -national, -racial, -generational, -genic, -species. The list could (and does) go on." The notion of trans- therefore seeks the transcending (*trans*-ing") of boundaries, be they disciplinary, theoretical, political, linguistic, or other. For more on the expressions "trans*" and "trans-," see Enke (2012a, 7, 19-20).

ible cis adjectives in feminist work, as Braithwaite and Orr demonstrate, allows for the destabilization of the universal cis identity as the foundation of feminism, to promote other perspectives of the world:

> As a result, becoming aware of what (and who) has been invisible means also becoming concerned with what (and who) is seen as neutral, universal and dominant, and, by default, what (and who) is considered biased and partisan, and thus is also negated. By situating knowledge in the world, we can both destabilize its likelihood of being taken-for-granted and use those new insights to understand, talk about, and potentially act in the world differently.[7]

The addition of the adjective (gender [identity]) to the title of Butler's *Gender Trouble* represents one of the visions allowing for the conceptualization of feminist and gender analyses from a new angle, inclusive of trans* people and favouring a renewal of feminist approaches at methodological, epistemological, and political levels.

This essay adopts a multi-methodological approach, or an approach that, while founded on theoretical analysis, nevertheless utilizes data deriving from quantitative and qualitative research conducted by other researchers, quantitative data collected for this research, and factual evidence collected through various trans* discussion lists and drawn from my own experience as a trans scholar working in feminist and gender studies (auto-ethnography). The thesis defended here posits that feminism has not only established itself as a field of study by marginalizing many people, such as racialized, socio-economically disadvantaged, lesbian, elderly, intersexed, or disabled women, but is also constructed on a cisgendernormativity[8] that excludes trans* subjects and produces gender

7 Braithwaite and Orr, *Everyday Women's and Gender Studies*, 18.

8 Baril, "Transsexualité et privilèges masculins. Fiction ou réalité?," 284. Baril coined the term "cisgendernormativity" to designate the normative aspect of the oppression of trans* people. He distinguishes "cisgendernormativity" from "cisgenderism" and notes that "cisgenderism is a system of oppression that affects trans* people, often called transphobia. It occurs on judicial, political, economic, social, medical, and normative levels. In this last case, we speak

analyses focusing predominantly on cisgender realities. While this cis presumption of gender is starting to be questioned by Anglophone feminists, as demonstrated by the recent proliferation of transfeminist[9] work, francophone feminists, with the few exceptions of trans* and feminist-identified people,[10] seem locked into

of 'cisgendernormativity'" (Baril, 2015a, 121).

9 Talia Mae Bettcher, "Feminist Perspectives on Trans Issues," Stanford Encyclopedia of Philosophy, Stanford University, 2006. http://plato.stanford.edu/entries/feminism-trans/; Pat Califa, Le mouvement transgenre. Changer de sexe, Translation by Patrick Ythier. Paris: EPEL, 2003; T. L. Cowan, "Transfeminist Kill/Joys: Rage, Love, and Reparative Performance," *TSQ: Transgender Studies Quarterly* 1, no. 4 (2014): 501-516; Anne Enke ed., *Transfeminist Perspectives In and Beyond Transgender and Gender Studies*, Philadelphia: Temple University Press (2012); Eli R. Green, "Debating Trans Inclusion in the Feminist Movement: A Trans-Positive Analysis," *Journal of Lesbian Studies* 10, no. 1/2 (2006): 231-248; Emi Koyama, "Transfeminist Manifesto," in *Catching a Wave: Reclaiming Feminism for the 21st Century*, 244-259, edited by Rory Dicker and Alison Piepmeier, Boston: Northeastern University Press, 2003; Emi Koyoma, "Whose Feminism Is It Anyway? The Unspoken Racism of the Trans Inclusion Debate," in *The Transgender Studies Reader*, 698-705, edited by Susan Stryker and Stephen Wittle, New York: Routledge 2006; Jean Bobby Noble, *Sons of the Movement: FtMs Risking Incoherence on a Post-Queer Cultural Landscape*, Toronto: Women's Press, 2006; Jean Bobby Noble, "Trans. Panic. Some Thoughts toward a Theory of Feminist Fundamentalism," in *Transfeminist Perspectives In and Beyond Transgender and Gender Studies*, 45- 59, edited by Anne Enke, Philadelphia: Temple University Press, 2012; Jack Pyne, "Transfeminist Theory and Action: Trans Women and the Contested Terrain of Women's Services," in *LGBTQ People and Social Work: Intersectional Perspectives*, 129-149, edited by Brian J O'Neil, Tracy A Swan, and Nick J. Mulé, Toronto: Canadian Scholars' Press 2015; Gayle Salamon, "Transfeminism and the Future of Gender," *Assuming a Body: Transgender and Rhetorics of Materiality*, New York, Columbia University Press (2010): 95-128; Krista Scott-Dixon ed., *Trans/Forming Feminisms: Trans/Feminist Voices Speak Out*, Toronto: Sumach Press, 2006; Julia Serano, *Whipping Girl: A Transsexual Woman on Sexism and the Scapegoating of Femininity*, Berkeley: Seal Press, 2007; Sandy Stone, "The Empire Strikes Back: A Posttranssexual Manifesto," in *The Transgender Studies Reader*, 221-236, edited by Susan Stryker and Stephen Wittle, New York, Routledge, 2006; Susan Stryker and Talia Bettcher, "Introduction: Trans/Feminisms," *TSQ: Transgender Studies Quarterly* 3, no. 1/2 (2016): 5-14; Stephen Whittle, "Where Did We Go Wrong? Feminism and Trans Theory: Two Teams on the Same Side?" in *The Transgender Studies Reader*, 194-202, edited by Susan Stryker and Stephen Whittle, New York: Routledge, 2006.

10 M.H./Sam Bourcier, "Des 'femmes travesties' aux pratiques trans-

a cisgendernormativity that remains invisible. This exclusion of trans* people is reflected in the composition of research teams dealing with trans* issues, feminist and gender studies programs and courses, and publications, to name just a few examples. This essay is therefore concerned with the systematic barriers that contribute to the exclusion of trans* people and prevent the decentring of the cis-centred subject in French Canadian academic feminism. This article aims to conduct a descriptive analysis of these structural obstacles, while suggesting potential solutions to overcome these limitations, most notably through a transfeminist approach. My goal is not to target specific departments, programs of study, or research teams, but to shed light on the structural dimension of cisgendernormativity cutting across Canadian academic institutions and research teams, especially in francophone communities,

---

genres: repenser et queeriser le travestissement," *CLIO, Histoire, femmes et sociétés* 10, (1999): 117-136; —, *Sexpolitiques: Queer zones 2*, Paris: La Fabrique, 2005; —, *Queer Zones. Politique des identités sexuelles et des savoirs,* Paris: Éditions Amsterdam, 2006; —, "Technotesto: biopolitiques des masculinités tr(s)ans hommes," *Cahiers du genre* 45, no. 2 (2008): 59-84; —, *Queer Zones 3. Identités, cultures et politiques*, Paris: Éditions Amsterdam, 2011. Alexandre Baril, "Transsexualité et privilèges masculins. Fiction ou réalité?"; —, "Quelle place pour les femmes trans au sein des mouvements féministes?," *Spirale* 247, (Winter 2014): 39-41; —, "Sexe et genre sous le bistouri (analytique): interprétations féministes des transidentités," *Recherches féministes* 28, no. 2 (2015): 121-141; —, "Francophone Trans/Feminisms: Absence, Silence, Emergence," *TSQ: Transgender Studies Quarterly* 3, no. 1/2 (2016): 40-47; —, "Intersectionality, Lost in Translation? (Re)thinking Inter-sections Between Anglophone and Francophone Intersectionality," *Atlantis: Critical Studies in Gender, Culture and Social Justice* 38, no. 1, (2017); M.H./Sam Bourcier, *et al.*, "Masculinités queer, trans et post-trans : les rejetons du féminisme: Entretiens croisés avec Carine Boeuf, Morty Diamond, Jin Haritaworn, Vincent He-say, Jean Bobby Noble et Stephen Whittle (propos recueillis par Marie-Hélène Bourcier et Pascale Molinier," *Cahiers du genre* 45, no. 2 (2008): 85-124; Karine Espineira, *La transidentité. De l'espace médiatique à l'espace public*, Paris : L'Harmattan, 2008; —, "Les constructions médiatiques des personnages trans. Un exemple d'inscription dans le programme 'penser le genre' en SIC," *Les enjeux de l'information et de la communication* 15, no. 1 (2014): 35-47; —, "Pour une épistémologie trans et féministe. Un exemple de production de savoirs situés," *Comment s'en sortir?* 2 (Fall 2015) : 42-58; —, *Transidentités: ordre et panique de genre*, Paris: L'Harmattan, 2015; —, Maud-Yeuse Thomas, et al., *Transféminismes, Cahiers de la transidentité,* no. 5, Paris: L'Harmattan, 2015.

preventing trans* people specializing in trans* issues, due to a glass ceiling phenomenon, to integrate academia and its higher ranks. This article invites all people working in academia to employ trans-inclusive practices and address the structural inequalities endured by trans* people, notably in feminist and gender studies.

This article is divided into three parts. The first section paints a portrait of cisgendernormativity in academic education and research across Canada. The second puts forward a case study of the francophone Canadian context to illustrate the near total absence of trans* issues in feminist teachings and works, despite a growing interest from students in such issues. In this section, I demonstrate that the paradox between students' growing interest and the lack of trans* university professors specializing in these issues is made possible by the exploitation of trans* people's unpaid and invisible labour. The third and concluding section utilizes a transfeminist approach and its notion of trans-ing to destabilize the cis-centrism of feminist and gender studies and to disrupt the disciplinary (sectarian) divisions contributing to the marginalization of trans* people in academia.

2. Cisgendernormativity in Academic Education and Research

The cisgendernormativity that dominates Canadian university education and research mirrors its prevalence in our society. Trans* people experience significant forms of discrimination, notably in the sphere of employment. A recent study conducted in the United States that included nearly 28,000 trans* people found that a majority of them experience forms of violence ranging from physical, psychological, and sexual violence to institutional and economic violence:

> The findings show large economic disparities between transgender people in the survey and the U.S. population. Nearly one-third (29%) of respondents were living in poverty, compared to 14% in the U.S. population. A major contributor to the high

> rate of poverty is likely respondents' 15% unemployment rate—three times higher than the unemployment rate in the U.S. population at the time of the survey (5%).[11]

The Canadian figures are similar: Shelley notes some studies report up to 40% of trans* people are unemployed[12] and Bauer and Scheim, who conducted one of the largest quantitative studies of Canadian trans* populations (433 subjects), show that many trans* people are laid off, not employed, and leave or decline certain jobs because their safety is compromised:

> Among trans Ontarians, 13% had been fired for being trans (another 15% were fired, and believed it might be because they were trans). Because they were trans, 18% were turned down for a job; another 32% suspected this was why they were turned down. Additionally, 17% declined a job they had applied for and were actually offered, because of the lack of a trans-positive and safe work environment. [13]

The consequences of such employment discrimination are substantial, since they trigger a cycle of poverty and social exclusion from which it is difficult to escape. These statistics are even more shocking when we consider that a majority of trans* people are qualified to work:

> Previous Trans PULSE findings showed that while 71% of trans people have at least some college or university education, about half make $15,000 per year or less. In light of this we sought to better understand the unique barriers to employment faced by trans Ontarians [...].[14]

---

11 Sandy E. James, *et al.*, *Executive Summary of the Report of the 2015 U.S. Transgender Survey*, (Washington, DC: National Center for Transgender Equality 2016), 3.

12 Christopher A. Shelley. *Transpeople: Repudiation, Trauma, Healing* (Toronto: University of Toronto Press, 2008), 82.

13 Greta R. Bauer and Ayden I. Scheim. *Transgender People in Ontario, Canada: Statistics from the Trans PULSE Project to Inform Human Rights Policy* (London, ON: The University of Western Ontario, 2015), 3.

14 Greta R. Bauer, *et al.*, "We've Got Work to Do: Workplace Discrimination and Employment Challenges for Trans People in Ontario," *Trans PULSE Bulletin Electronique* 2, no. 1 (2011), 1.

Trans* women are especially vulnerable because of the simultaneous presence of both sexism and cisgenderism (or "cissexism"[15]): when they are not laid off or denied employment, their salaries, like that of other women, are affected. Based on their quantitative study, Schilt and Wiswall conclude, "In becoming women, MTFs experience significant losses in hourly earnings."[16] The testimonies of many trans* people confirm these types of discrimination, such as that of Lalla Kowska-Régnier, who was laid off and whose salary decreased following her transition: "I would add that my professional projects were interrupted, notably because my ex-future employers became aware of my transition [...]. Today, since I got fired, my [...] income has been divided by nearly 3...and I remain in a pretty precarious situation."[17]

The academic world is nothing but a reflection of our societies. It is plagued by the same -isms (heterosexism, racism, colonialism, ableism, cisgenderism, etc.) shaping its structures and systems of operation. It is thus possible to think that discrimination experienced by trans* people in the general workforce also exists in the university setting.[18] Though no quantitative data exists pertaining to discrimination experienced by trans* people attempting to obtain professorships in Canadian universities, I will demonstrate herein that trans* professors are under-represented, a reality linked to cisgenderist discrimination. While many trans* researchers in academia work in a diverse range of fields, including biology, economics, and communications, some, like other marginalized people, choose to specialize in fields which take up questions concerning their identities and oppression. *Yet trans* experts, specializing*

15 Julia Serano, *Whipping Girl.*

16 Kristen Schilt, and Matthew Wiswall, "Before and After: Gender Transition, Human Capital, and Workplace Experiences," *The B.E. Journal of Economic Analysis and Policy* 8, no. 1 (2008), 2.

17 Lalla Kowska-Régnier, "Trans féminisme ou Transinisme?," (2009), 2. https://www.minorites.org/index.php/2-la-revue/375-trans-feminisme-ou-transinisme.html. Retrieved February 11th, 2010.

18 Alex Hanna, "Being Transgender on the Job Market," *Inside Higher Ed.*, (2016), https://www.insidehighered.com/advice/2016/07/15/challenge-being-transgender-academic-jobmarket-essay. Retrieved April 13th, 2016.

in trans studies, only occupy twelve positions*[19] *in Canadian university departments*. Despite the new laws on trans* rights, the transformation of public and institutional politics pertaining to trans* issues (including at universities) and the increased presence of trans* people in the media and in social spheres, in 2018, only twelve self-identified trans* people specializing in trans* issues hold permanent professor positions in all of Canada.

Notions of direct and indirect discrimination held dear by feminists shed light on the absence of trans* experts in academia. We know that trans* people in certain sectors are laid off or denied employment due to their identities, which constitutes direct discrimination. Nevertheless, as stressed by feminists, indirect discrimination is omnipresent and often more difficult to prove.[20] For several decades, for example, the fact that some women had less

19 These data are not derived from a quantitative study. Nevertheless, since the field of trans* studies is limited within the Canadian context, all people working in this field can be located. During my research, I have come across only eleven self-identified trans* experts across Canada who hold a permanent or tenure-track position (research conducted in 2017). In January 2018, when I officially started my position as assistant professor at the School of Social Work at the University of Ottawa, I therefore became the twelfth trans person and the first francophone trans person in Canada to be hired as a professor specializing in trans* issues and teach this content in French. Some trans* people occupy permanent positions, *but they do not publicly self-identify as trans* and/or do not work on questions pertaining to trans* issues*, as is the case with Alex Hanna (2016), professor of communication studies at the University of Toronto, who is openly trans* but does not specialize in trans* studies. The majority of people who self-identify as trans* and who specialize in trans* issues do not hold permanent positions, despite their qualifications and search for work. The eleven aforementioned trans* experts work at the University of Victoria, Royal Roads University, Queen's University (two professors), York University (three professors), Carleton University, Concordia University, McGill University and the University of New Brunswick. This data has been verified by the majority of these professors and by several other people in trans* studies (who do not occupy permanent positions). There are also a few additional academics in Canada specializing in trans* issues, *but these people are not trans**.

20 Huguette Dagenais ed., "La vie quotidienne des professeures d'université," (Montreal: Fédération québécoise des professeures et professeurs d'université [FQPPU], 1996), 71; Louise Boucher, "L'embauche des femmes professeures dans les universités : résistances et stratégies," (Montreal: FQPPU, 1996).

extensive CVs than their male counterparts, since they carried out most unpaid and invisible labour in the private sphere, was not interpreted as a form of indirect discrimination nor as a factor preventing women from gaining access to academic positions. The implementation of affirmative action programs has begun to address these systemic inequalities, taking into consideration the time women must invest when they have children and the ensuing repercussions on their careers.[21] As I have demonstrated elsewhere,[22] many trans* people experience particular temporalities and delays in their careers attributable to surgeries, convalescence, recurring doctors' appointments, civil identity change procedures, etc., but these delays are never taken into consideration during hiring processes. Nevertheless, many trans* people who have been pregnant maintain that these factors can be compared to a pregnancy in terms of their duration. This argument is supported by Raewyn Connell's discussion of the "work of transition" and the time it requires.[23] The violence perpetuated in the educational milieu that leads some trans* people to abandon their studies must also be considered, as must the financial difficulties faced by trans* people due to economic discrimination,[24] which prevent some trans* people

21 Ibid.

22 Alexandre Baril, "Transness as Debility: Rethinking Intersections between Trans and Disabled Embodiments," *Feminist Review* 111 (2015): 59-74; —, "'Doctor, am I an Anglophone trapped in a Francophone body?' An Intersectional Analysis of 'Trans-crip-t Time' in Ableist, Cisnormative, Anglonormative Societies," *Journal of Literary and Cultural Disability Studies* 10, no. 2 (2016): 155-172.; —, "Temporalité trans : identité de genre, temps transitoire et éthique médiatique," *Enfances, familles, générations: Revue internationale* 25, (2017).

23 Raewyn Connell, "Transsexual Women and Feminist Thought: Toward New Understanding and New Politics," *Signs* 37, no. 4 (2012), 870.

24 Bauer, Greta, *et al.* "We've Got Work to Do: Workplace Discrimination and Employment Challenges for Trans People in Ontario," *Trans PULSE Bulletin Electronique* 2, no. 1 (2011), 1-2. Bauer, Greta R. and Ayden I. Scheim. *Trangerder People in Ontario, Canada: Statistics from the Trans PULSE Project to Inform Human Rights Policy*, London, Ontario, The University of Western Ontario, 2015. Chamberland, Line, Alexandre Baril, and Natalie Duchesne. *La transphobie en milieu scolaire au Québec : rapport de recherche*, Montréal: UQAM, 2011. James, Sandy E., *et al. Executive Summary of the Report of the 2015 U.S. Transgender Survey*, Washington: National Center for Transgender Equality, 2016. OHRC (Ontario

from pursuing academic paths and applying for certain positions.

Furthermore, Canada's employment equity laws list four groups whose oppressive social conditions have prevented full participation in the work force: Indigenous people, visible minorities, disabled people, and women.[25] It is possible that, with the establishment of new legislation such as Bill C-16 (a law modifying Canadian human rights law and the Criminal Code), trans* people will be included among these discriminated groups but, as I write this article, this is not the case. Thus, the majority of Canadian universities, even when they take the inequalities experienced by members of these four groups seriously and implement procedures to identify them during the hiring process—having applied to about forty positions this year, I can confirm that nearly half of the universities did not send out self-identification forms regarding the four groups, though they claim to subscribe to employment equity principles—do not include gender identity as a potential negative impact on one's career, though this can evidently be the case. Let us consider the following example: on the self-identification form sent to me by a few universities, I was given the option of choosing between either "man" or "woman." As I am legally a man, I checked off "man," a choice that erases the 27 years I lived with the identity of "woman," which shaped the person I am today, as well as my career (e.g., the opportunities I was granted or denied).[26] In short, this choice conceals the sexism I experienced throughout these decades, while dismissing the combined effects of cisgenderism and sexism. Does the following not constitute a double standard? Having experienced systemic sexism with poten-

---

Human Rights Commission). *Policy on Preventing Discrimination Because of Gender Identity and Gender Expression*, Toronto: Human Rights Commission, 2014. Schilt, Kristen, et Matthew Wiswall. "Before and After: Gender Transitions, Human Capital, and Workplace Experiences," *The B.E. Journal of Economic Analysis and Policy* 8, no. 1 (2008): 1-26. Shelley, Christopher A. *Transpeople: Repudiation, Trauma, Healing*. Toronto: University of Toronto Press, 2008.

25 Government of Canada, "Employment Equity Act," 2017, https://laws-lois.justice.gc.ca/eng/acts/e-5.401/page-1.html.

26 Jean Bobby Noble, *Sons of the Movement*, 58. Noble discusses the erasure of trans* men's past histories as women.

tial negative impacts on their careers, two people apply for a job. One person (a cis woman) benefits from affirmative action, while the other person (a trans* man assigned female at birth) may not take advantage of these measures nor even indicate the cisgenderist structural obstacles impeding their career.

Indirect discrimination is not limited to the lack of consideration of cisgenderism in hiring processes nor to the absence of affirmative action measures for trans* people in employment equity laws; it also acts on the epistemological level in academia, that is to say, on the level of knowledge considered valid and scientific.[27] Indirect discrimination can therefore derive from departmental decision-making processes that may seem, at first glance, to be neutral and objective (e.g., determining fields of specialization and hiring of professors, courses and seminars to be offered, and so on), but which are strongly influenced by the above-mentioned -isms, including cisgenderism. Consider the following example: the first academic feminists were refused employment, despite having qualifications equivalent or superior to their male colleagues, not necessarily because they were women (direct discrimination) but because their areas of specialization (women and feminism) were viewed as being very specific compared to the supposedly universal research of their male colleagues.[28] In short, it seemed more important in the 1970s and 1980s (and still often seems so) for a department to hire a fifth sociology of culture expert than a single expert on gender. The history of this indirect discrimination is repeated with respect to other marginalized groups, notably trans* people: despite a growing student interest in trans* issues, hiring in fields of specialization outside those addressing trans* issues is of higher priority (as demonstrated by the fact that only twelve trans* people specializing in trans* issues occupy tenured or tenure-track

27 Karine Espineira, "Pour une épistémologie trans et féministe", 42-58.

28 Huguette Dagenais, "L'institutionnalisation des études feminists et la transformation des connaissances et de leurs conditions de production ou Pour en finir avec un faux débat," ed. Pierrette Bouchard, *Les Cahiers de recherche du GREMF: Femmes et savoirs*, Actes du *Congrès de l'ACFAS* "Femmes et savoirs," (Québec: Université Laval, 1995).

positions in Canada), while departments often already employ experts in the field for which they are hiring. In other words, the privileging of a specific field, rather than being understood as a form of indirect discrimination stemming from a concrete ideological and normative cis-centred system, is often perceived as a departmental preference.

In response to this argument, some people might be inclined to present the counter-argument that the trans* population in Canada represents but a miniscule percentage of the total population. If we consider the most recent statistics, however, trans* people represent close to 0.5% of the population.[29] By comparison, incarcerated people in Canada represent 0.14% (139/100,000).[30] The trans* population is therefore almost four times larger than the incarcerated population, and yet Canadian criminology departments are quite vast in terms of number of faculty. Of the hundreds of criminology professors, many specialize in prisons and incarceration, yet no one seems to question the fact that this minority group makes up a smaller portion of the general population than does the trans* population. I am not critiquing the number of criminologists and academics specializing in prisons and incarceration (several hundred in Canada), who tackle important topics (trans* people experience considerably higher rates of incarceration than the rest of the population; Scheim, *et al.* note that 6% of trans* people in Canada have been incarcerated).[31] Neither am I arguing that any particular issue's significance should depend on a quantitative dimension. Rather, my objective is to highlight

29 Travis William Davidson, "A Review of Transgender Health in Canada," *University of Ottawa Journal of Medicine* 5, no. 2 (2015), 41; Greta R. Bauer and Ayden I. Scheim. *Transgender People in Ontario, Canada*; Anne Enke "Introduction: Transfeminist Perspectives and Note on Terms and Concepts," in *Transfeminist Perspectives In and Beyond Transgender and Gender Studies*, edited by Anne Enke, (Philadelphia: Temple University Press, 2012), 1-20.

30 Alter Justice, "Le taux d'incarcération au Canada et au Québec," (2017), http://www.alterjustice.org/dossiers/statistiques/taux-incarceration.html. Retrieved on February 13th, 2017.

31 Ayden Scheim, *et al*, "Les experiences de prison des participants de Trans PULSE et des recommandations de changement," *Trans PULSE Bulletin Electronique* 3, no. 3 (2013).

the fact that very few people question the relevance of hiring more experts on prisons and incarceration, while many do question the relevance of opening positions for experts on trans* issues on the pretense that the trans* population represents a very small minority of people. The refusal to consider expertise on trans* issues as relevant in sociology, criminology, political science, literature, and even feminist and gender studies, or the refusal to consider the trans* category in affirmative action measures, constitutes forms of indirect discrimination (in addition to direct discrimination) founded on a cis-centred, epistemic violence excluding trans* people from academia.

2.1 Research on Trans* People or Research by/for Trans* People?

> Until recently, the overwhelming majority of scholarship building the field of transgender studies was produced by people who worked outside, or in marginal positions within, the academy: activists, graduate students, and people in temporary positions. The balance is only beginning to shift (but not yet tip), with an increasing number of scholars who have secure (tenure-track and tenured) positions in academic institutions [...].[32]

If, as Enke indicates, the United States is experiencing its first wave of employment of trans* experts in trans* issues, this is not the case in Canada, where only twelve such experts have been hired in tenure-track positions. Canadian trans* people remain confined to precarious positions (research assistants, lecturers, professors with limited-term appointment, etc.) In this section, I will demonstrate that the growing body of Canadian research in trans* studies is predominantly conducted by cisgender professors and researchers. The distinction between research *on* trans* people and *by/for* trans* people may seem unimportant, but it is not, as anti-oppressive studies note. While it would be seen as problematic if a major-

32 Anne Enke, "Introduction: Transfeminist Perspectives and Note on Terms and Concepts," 8-9.

ity of feminist research was conducted by cisgender men, or if a majority of critical race research was conducted by white people, the fact that the majority of trans* research is currently conducted by cisgender people does not seem to cause any outrage. Like authors who suggest that this attitude stems from a sense of entitlement founded on cis privilege,[33] I believe that many (not all) cis Canadian researchers feel justified in leading subsidised research *on* trans* people and trans* realities without questioning the space they occupy as cis people in this field.

In October 2016, I participated in consultations conducted by the Advisory Board of Canada's Fundamental Science Review, which were mandated by Minister of science Kirsty Duncan to discuss systematic barriers affecting certain marginalized groups in academic research, particularly with respect to their careers and funding (Canadian Institute of Health Research (CIHR); Natural Sciences and Engineering Research Council of Canada (NSERC); Social Sciences and Humanities Research Council of Canada (SSHRC)). I have done extensive research on the funding of research on trans* issues (2011-15) and have shown that trans* people receive little funding, and that research on trans* realities is predominantly led by cis people and conducted in English. Here is some of the data collected from grant agency websites about the most prestigious sources of funding in Canada: [34]

33 Julia Serano, *Whipping Girl*; Alexandre Baril, "Transsexualité et privilèges masculins. Fiction ou réalité ?"; Evin Taylor, "Cisgender Privilege: On the Privileges of Performing Normative Gender," in *Gender Outlaws: Next Generation*, 268-272, Eds. Kate Bornstein and S. Bear Bergman (Berkeley: Seal Press, 2010).

34 This research was conducted using grant agency search engines in October 2016, utilizing the keywords "transgender," "transsexual," and variations thereof (e.g., transsex* for transsexuality, etc.) in both English and French, to search keywords or titles of research projects. The application years included, unless otherwise indicated, from 2010-11 to 2014-15, data from five consecutive years (2011, 2012, 2013, 2014, 2015). Projects on trans* issues may not have been considered if their titles or keywords did not include the aforementioned terms. Results provided by the SSHRC search engine are presented year-by-year; a project granted funding over a three-year period would therefore appear three times. These duplicates have been removed.

Canada Excellence Research Chairs

- No (0) chairs on trans* issues.

Canada Research Chairs Program (CRCP), including CIHR, NSERC, and SSHRC (Tiers 1 and 2)

- Of over 1800 chairs, none (0) contain, in title or keywords, the terms transsexual, transgender, or their variations.
- Of over 1800 chairs, only three (3) (Anglophone) chairs contain, in their summaries, the terms transsexual, transgender, or any variation thereof (Sexual and Gender Minority Studies, Philosophy of Gender and Sexuality, Indigenous Literature and Expressive Culture). While the last chair does not deal primarily with questions of gender or sexuality, the first two integrate these issues significantly. Nevertheless, neither of the two chairholders self-identify as trans* and, at the time of writing, their funded work does not deal primarily with trans* issues.
- In Canada, there are only two (2) research chairs interested in trans* issues: the Chair in Transgender Studies (University of Victoria) dedicated to trans* issues and led by a trans* researcher, and the Chaire de recherche sur l'homophobie (Chair of Research on Homophobia) (UQAM), focusing on LGBT issues and led by a person who does not self-identify as trans*. However, these chairs are not CRCs, and their funding derives from private sources in the first case and from a combination of funding sources in the second.

Banting Postdoctoral Fellowships (2012-2017)[35]

- None (0) of the 424 CIHR-, NSERC-, and SSHRC-awarded grants contain, in their titles or keywords, the terms transsexual, transgender, or their variations.

SSHRC Postdoctoral Fellowships

- Only four (4) of the 3133 awarded grants contain, in their titles

35 Since Banting scholarships only became available in 2012 (there is therefore no data for 2011), the present research includes the year 2016-17 (instead of concluding with 2015-16) to obtain statistics for a five-year period, in accordance with the rest of the data presented here. The same method is applied with respect to the Vanier Canada Graduate Scholarships.

or keywords, the terms transsexual, transgender, or their variations.

- Only one (1) of these grants was awarded to a French-language project.

SSHRC Doctoral Fellowships

- Only fifteen (15) of the 2674 awarded grants contain, in their titles or keywords, the terms transsexual, transgender, or their variations.
- Only one (1) of these grants was awarded to a French-language project.

SSHRC Doctoral Fellowships from the Canada Graduate Scholarships Program

- Only eight (8) of the 2281 awarded grants contain, in their titles or keywords, the terms transsexual, transgender, or their variations.
- Only one (1) of these grants was awarded to a French-language project.

Vanier Canada Graduate Scholarships (SSHRC Stream, 2012-2017)

- Only four (4) of the 276 awarded grants contain, in their titles or keywords, the terms transsexual, transgender, or their variations.[36]

SSHRC Grants: Insight Development Grants for Single Researchers, Research Teams, and Partnerships[37]

- Only ten (10) grants awarded to English-language projects contain, in their titles or keywords, the terms transsexual, transgender, or their variations. The majority of these projects are not

36 The results of the 2016-17 competition revealed that two new chairholders are now dealing with trans* issues in their projects, using the terms "non-binary," and "gender minorities."

37 The results presented above combine all the grants included under the "Insight Program" tab of the SSHRC search engine. Though the precise number of awarded grants is not directly accessible through the search engine, it totals in the several thousands when no search term is entered.

conducted by self-identified trans* people.

- Only two (2) grants awarded to French-language projects contain, in their titles or keywords, the terms transsexual, transgender, or their variations. Neither of these two projects is conducted by self-identified trans* people.

When we include the LGBT acronym in our research on SSHRC's grants, a few more results appear (the difference remains insignificant). Still, we cannot forget, as emphasized by Stryker (2008), Namaste (2000, 2005, 2015), and Connell (2012), that a great majority of the research concerning LGBT populations focuses on lesbian, gay, and bisexual issues. In short, this focus on sexuality issues often does not entail a complete or profound discussion of trans* issues. In fact, sexual identity (or sexual orientation), though related to gender identity, is a fundamentally different issue. Many trans* researchers question the underlying "tokenism" of this grouping of trans* people with sexual minorities, which allows cisgender researchers a clear conscience in relation to trans* issues and permits them to secure research funding. As noted by Kowska-Régnier, "In other words, in my own life I prefer the term 'trans' because 'trans,' when it stands on its own, does not drown me in an ocean of queerness, and yet allows me to inscribe myself in a collective space. I have had enough of the LGBT narrative in which the T has only ever stood for: Ticket for the clear conscience of the G!"[38] While this critique does not apply to every person researching LGBT issues, since some do, out of ethical concerns, include trans* people as co-researchers and/or research assistants on their team, it does reflect an all too pervasive reality. In short, as the figures presented here demonstrate, the few funded research projects in Canada dealing with trans* realities are almost exclusively English-language projects, and are conducted primarily by cis people.

2.2 Trans* Studies Within Feminism: Between Absence and Presence[39]

38 Kowska-Régnier, "Trans féminisme ou Transinisme?," 3.

39 The expression "between absence and presence" is borrowed from Ru-

In her book, *Oversight: Critical Reflections on Feminist Research and Politics,* Viviane Namaste introduces the polysemic concept of oversight. This term designates both that which is omitted, concealed, and absent, as well as that which is simultaneously present and hyper-visible, through processes of surveillance/vigilance. Namaste writes,

> I use the term [oversight] in two specific ways. First, the notion of oversight refers to that which has been ignored—the day-to-day realities that remain unexplored by scholars and activists, the stories that have yet to be told. […] Here, oversight is used to designate what has yet to be made visible. Yet I also use *oversight* in a second sense, specifically to refer to understanding the ways in which what appears visible has been overdetermined by specific social, activist, cultural, and economic contexts. Here, then, the focus is not on what cannot be seen. Rather, the idea is to interrogate how and why issues are made visible, in particular ways, within feminist academic and scholarly contexts.[40]

The notion of oversight can be understood as a practice of erasure and occultation (absence), as well as one of (hyper)-visibilization when considering trans* issues from a specific ideological/epistemological lens (presence). I will demonstrate how this logic is the result of the presumption of mutual exclusivity between trans perspectives and feminist and gender studies, stemming from a cisgendernormativity that leaves the feminist cisgender subject unchallenged.

The presence of trans* issues in cultural representations and in the media is, as of a few years ago, increasingly common: from the coming out of Caitlyn Jenner to that of Chaz Bono, from Janet Mook's autobiographies to the television series featuring Laverne Cox, and from the media coverage of the changing laws concerning trans* rights to the public demands issued by transactivist movements, trans* issues appear to be in vogue.[41] Increasing

bin "Trans Studies: Between a Metaphysics of Presence and Absence."

40 Viviane Namaste, *Oversight: Critical Reflections on Feminist Research and Politics* (Toronto: Women's Press, 2015), 1-2.

41 Julia Serano, *Whipping Girl*; Karine Espineira, *La transidentité. De l'espace médiatique à l'espace public*; —, "Les constructions médiatiques des personnages

numbers of trans* people are also gaining visibility in academia and demanding that their rights be respected, calling for gender-neutral bathrooms, access to trans-inclusive campus health services, or for their preferred name(s) and pronouns to be respected in their classes. In Canadian feminist and gender studies departments, committees are forming to discuss trans-inclusive practices, to make certain spaces (such as washrooms) accessible for trans* people, and to create new courses on trans* issues in order to meet the growing demand from students. Over the last few years, as reflected by the decision of the Canadian Women's Studies Association/Association Canadienne des études sur les femmes to change its name to Women's and Gender Studies/Recherches Féministes Association (WGSRF) to be more inclusive, most departments have been changing their names. While most of these departments initially called themselves Women's Studies departments, the opposite is now true: out of a total of 48 departments, only nine (19%) have yet to change their names to include "gender studies," "sexuality studies," etc.[42] In other words, 81% of feminist studies departments in Canada have jumped on the "gender bandwagon" by changing the names of their departments, programs, and courses. Though one could interpret this turning point as a sign of structural change, allowing for a departure from those types of feminist studies that only consider the (cis) woman subject, as the near total absence of self-identified trans* tenured professors specializing in trans* issues in these departments demonstrates, this is clearly not the case. *In fact, only three departments include such experts*: Concordia University, Queen's University, and York University. The relative absence of trans* professors specializing in trans* issues would be

trans"; Susan Stryker, Paisley Currah, and Lisa Jean Moore, "Introduction: Trans-, Trans, or Transgender?"; Alexandre Baril, "Temporalité trans : identité de genre, temps transitoire et éthique médiatique," *Enfances, familles, générations: Revue internationale* 25, (2017).

42 The list of departments can be found on the WGSRF webpage (2017). The nine departments are at the University of Calgary, University of the Fraser Valley, Vancouver Island University, Mount Saint Vincent University, Lakehead University, University of Waterloo, University of Western Ontario, Concordia University, and the Université du Québec à Montréal.

understandable if their absence was due to an absence of trans* scholars overall, but this is not the case: many trans* scholars are actively looking for work but are confined to precarious positions. In short, if Canadian feminist and gender studies departments include only three trans* professors specializing in these issues, it is because, despite seemingly trans-inclusive gestures such as the changes made to their department names, programs, and courses (gestures of presence/visibility), the implementation of trans-inclusive policies allowing for the development of trans* perspectives through the prioritization of specialization in trans* studies and the employment of trans* people, for example, remains limited.

Jean Bobby Noble demonstrates that even those departments employing trans* people have yet to abandon cis-centred perspectives, which present themselves through "micropractices" (e.g., the feminization of all departmental documents without considering trans* people, course offerings, or strategic departmental directions). Noble writes,

> If I were to ask any ten feminist academics in and across my home university whether trans bodies are present, or should be, as trans bodies in women's studies, [...] I cannot help but worry that the answer will be a quiet or completely dumbfounded no, even in the face of my hire.[43]

Even in the United States, where cisgendernormativity is starting to be challenged, feminist and gender studies continue to conceive specialization in the field of trans* studies as exterior to their own objects of study, methodologies, and epistemologies, thereby demonstrating the cis-centred character of the notion of "gender."[44][45]

43 Jean Bobby Noble, "Trans. Panic, Some Thoughts toward a Theory of Feminist Fundamentalism," 47.

44 Sara E. Cooper, and Connor James Treba, "Teaching Transgender in Women's Studies: Snarls and Strategies," *Journal of Lesbian Studies* 10, no.1/2 (2006): 151-180; Toby Beauchamp and Benjamin d'Harlingue, "Beyond Additions and Exceptions: The Category of Transgender and New Pedagogical Approaches for Women's Studies," *Feminist Formations* 24, no. 2 (2012): 25-51; T. L. Cowan, "Transfeminist Kill/Joys."

45 For more on the feminist and trans* studies debates, see: Alexandre Baril, "Transsexualité et privilèges masculins. Fiction ou réalité ?"; —. "Quelle

Enke writes,

> Nevertheless, transgender remains institutionally marginal to gender and women's studies. As a well-established field, gender and women's studies may include transgender as an add-on, without fundamentally changing the theoretical articulations and material practices that all but ensure that the definition of 'women's studies' will position transgender as something outside or other than itself. [...] Transgender studies is all but absent in most university curricula, even in gender and women's studies programs. For the most part, institutionalized versions of women's and gender studies incorporate transgender as a shadowy interloper or as the most radical outlier within a constellation of identity categories (e.g., LGBT). Conversation is limited by a

place pour les femmes trans au sein des mouvements féministes?"; —, "Sexe et genre sous le bistouri (analytique)"; —, "Intersectionality, Lost in Translation?"; Patricia Elliott, *Debates in Transgender, Queer, and Feminist Theory: Contested Sites*, Farnham, Ashgate, 2010; Eli R. Green, "Debating Trans Inclusion in the Feminist Movement: A Trans-Positive Analysis"; Cressida J. Heyes "Reading Transgender, Rethinking Women's Studies," *NWSA Journal* 12, no. 2 (2000): 170-180; —, "Feminist Solidarity after Queer Theory: The Case of Transgender," *Signs* 28, no. 4 (2003): 1093-1120; Graham Mayeda, "Re-imagining Feminist Theory: Transgender Identity, Feminism, and the Law," *Canadian Journal of Women and the Law/Revue femmes et droit*, no. 42 (2005): 423-472; —; Viviane Namaste, *Sex Change, Social Change: Reflections on Identity, Institutions, and Imperialism*, Toronto: Women's Press, 2005; —. "Undoing Theory: The 'Transgender Question' and the Epistemic Violence of Anglo-American Feminist Theory," *Hypatia* 24, no. 3 (2009): 11-32; Viviane Namaste and Georgia Sitara, "Inclusive Pedagogy in the Women's Studies Classroom: Teaching the Kimberly Nixon Case," in *The Transgender Studies Reader* 2, 213-225, edited by Susan Stryker and Aren Z. Aizura. New York: Routledge, 2013; Jack Pyne, "Transfeminist Theory and Action"; Gayle Salamon, "Transfeminism and the Future of Gender"; Julia Serano, *Whipping Girl*; —, *Excluded. Making Feminist and Queer Movements More Inclusive*. Berkeley: Seal Press, 2013; Susan Stryker, "Transgender Feminism: Queering the Woman Question," in *Third Wave Feminism: A Critical Exploration*, 59-70, edited by Stacy Gillis, Gillian Howie and Rebecca Munford, New York, Palgrave MacMillan, 2007; Amélie Tremblay, "Trans-formation féministe: l'univers d'un homme transsexuel féministe. Entretien avec Alexandre Baril," in *Remous, ressacs et dérivations autour de la troisième vague féministe*, 93-111, edited by Mercédès Baillargeon and collectif Les Déferlantes. Montréal : Les éditions du Remue-ménage, 2011; Stephen Whittle, "Where Did We Go Wrong? Feminism and Trans Theory."

> perception that transgender studies only or primarily concerns transgender-identified individuals—a small number of 'marked' people whose gender navigations are magically believed to be separate from the cultural practices that constitute gender for everyone else.[46]

My emphasis herein on the cisgender and unmarked "invisible adjectives" that populate the texts, courses, and programs of study on gender, as well as the epistemological and political orientations of feminist and gender studies departments, aims to question the position of exteriority maintained by gender and feminist studies since their conception of trans* perspectives, which, while benefiting from a hyper-visibility, also remains missing from the feminist portrait. While this absence is disconcerting and increasingly studied by Anglophone transfeminist authors, it is flagrant in the francophone community and remains unproblematized.

3. Trans* Studies and Research in French Canada

Despite the increasing visibility of trans* people and their calls to action in the public sphere, the marked interest of students in trans* issues, and the efforts of francophone feminists to adopt an intersectional approach in their work and teaching philosophies in order to include more diverse groups of women,[47] Namaste's phenomenon of oversight is rampant in French-Canadian feminism.[48] As mentioned elsewhere, in my analyses of feminist publications on intersectionality,[49] francophone feminists have yet to include

46 Enke, Anne. "Introduction: Transfeminist Perspectives and Note on Terms and Concepts," 2.

47 Sirma Bilge, "Théorisations féministes de l'intersectionnalité," *Diogène* 225, (2009): 70-88; Alexandre Baril, "Sexe et genre sous le bistouri (analytique): interprétations féministes des transidentités"; Geneviève Pagé, and Rosa Pires, *L'intersectionnalité en débat: pour un renouvellement des pratiques féministes au Québec*, Montréal: Service aux collectivités de l'UQAM/Fédération des femmes du Québec, 2015.

48 Namaste, *Oversight: Critical Reflections on Feminist Research and Politics*.

49 Baril, "Intersectionality, Lost in Translation?"; —, "Francophone

trans* identity and oppression on their list of identities or forms of oppression:

> In a sample of 15 key Francophone texts on feminism and intersectionality, only one makes a single mention of trans issues amidst lengthy enumerations of other oppressions. Simply stated [...] Francophone feminists seem to forget that they have a gender identity [...].[50]

In light of the data presented above, it would not be an exaggeration to suggest that studies *by/for* trans* people in French-Canadian scholarship are non-existent; though only eleven trans* professors specializing in trans* issues are employed across Canada, at the time of writing, none of them were teaching in the French language.[51] This situation will change slightly when I begin my appointment, in January 2018, as a francophone assistant professor at the School of Social Work at the University of Ottawa teaching, most notably, content related to sexual, gender, and body diversity. The situation in the international francophone community is not much brighter. In France, for example, where a few self-identified trans* experts on trans* issues can be found (such as Karine Espineira)[52] only Sam Bourcier[53] occupies a tenured position, and obtained it prior to transitioning and prior to his more marked interest in trans* issues. In the following pages, I will demonstrate that the total absence of trans* francophone professors in Canada is problematic given the marked interest of students in trans* issues and is made possible thanks to the exploitation of trans* people's unpaid and invisible labour.

Trans/Feminisms: Absence, Silence, Emergence."

50 Baril, "Intersectionality, Lost in Translation?", 2-3.

51 Although Namaste is bilingual, she teaches at an English-language university.

52 Karine Espineira, *La transidentité. De l'espace médiatique à l'espace public*; —, "Les constructions médiatiques des personnages trans"; —, "Pour une épistémologie trans et féministe"; —, *Transidentités : ordre et panique de genre.*

53 M.H./Sam Bourcier, "Des 'femmes travesties' aux pratiques transgenres"; —, *Sexpolitiques: Queer Zones* 2; —, *Queer Zones. Politique des identités sexuelles et des savoirs.* —, "Technotesto: biopolitiques des masculinités tr(s)ans hommes," —, *Queer Zones* 3. *Identités, cultures et politiques.*

3.1 Students' Growing Interest in Trans* Issues

> In recent years, we have noticed important developments in trans* research at UQAM. More and more students are interested in such questions and are conducting research on this subject, and this trend will likely continue to progress in this direction.[54]

The growing interest of students in trans* issues can be observed on many levels. I myself have noticed it in my classes (as a teaching assistant or limited-term contract professor), and it has been brought to my attention by several colleagues. This enthusiasm can also be observed in the constant requests I have received over the last five years to co-supervise major research projects/theses on trans* issues, the significant number of students present at conferences on trans* issues, the submissions of departmental student committee reports denouncing the absence of trans* issues in courses,[55] and in the use of published research concerning trans* issues. Using social media platforms like Academia.edu, we see that the works of trans* francophone scholars such as Bourcier (more than 33, 500 profile views) and Baril (more than 30, 200 profile views) are highly sought after; these two scholars' profiles have remained, for over a year and half, in the top 0.5-1% of the most visited by the website's 58 million users.[56]

This interest in trans* issues is also confirmed by quantitative studies, such as that of the UQAM research chair on homophobia.[57] Using over sixty keywords on sexual and gender diversity, this research identified and reviewed all the Québec universities theses

54 Michael Chacha Enriquez, *et al*, "Développer les études trans dans la francophonie : pésentation de quelques résultats et enjeux issus de deux recherches utiles aux communautés trans," *Convergence : A Journal of Undergraduate and Community Research* 1 (September 2012), 100.

55 Comité féministe des deuxième et troisième cycles de sociologie de l'UQAM, 2017.

56 These data have been updated for the publication of this translation.

57 Marie Geoffroy and Mahault Albarracin, *Mémoires et Thèses reliés à l'homophobie et à la pluralité des genres paurus au Québec de 2000 à 2014*, (Montréal : Chaire de recherche sur l'homophobie, UQAM, 2015).

and dissertations addressing LGBT themes submitted between 2000 and 2015. This research, titled "Mémoires et thèses reliés à l'homophobie" ("Theses and Dissertations on Homophobia") in 2014, was revisited in 2015, "[...] in order to be more representative of the themes addressed."[58] It is now titled "Mémoires et thèses reliés à l'homophobie et à la pluralité des genres" ("Theses and Dissertations Related to Sexual Diversity and *the Plurality of Genders*") (emphasis added). The review identified 238 texts on sexual and gender diversity, including 60 doctoral dissertations, 166 master's projects, and 12 other texts, a high number given how few people are employed in universities to work on such topics. Based on the titles of these texts, I have identified 37 texts (32 dissertations and 5 theses) out of 238 (15.5%) linked to trans* issues.[59] Irrespective of other works unaccounted for by this research (research conducted in databases is never exhaustive), it is astounding to find no francophone trans* professors specializing in trans* issues at any Canadian university and to realize that *these projects and theses are supervised by cis people, most of whom do not specialize in trans* studies.* The UQAM report included a published list of the 107 professors who supervised these projects. With the exception of one trans* person on this list (whom I know personally), who has neither publicly self-identified as trans* nor specializes in trans* issues, all of these professors are self-identified or publicly identified cis people. Would we not find it strange if a list of 238 theses and projects on job inequality, including 15.5% percent that focused on inequalities experienced by women, were supervised by 107 men? It would be interesting to reflect critically on these lists and on who is absent or excluded from them.

3.2 The Absence of Gender Identity in Francophone Feminist Research and Education

58 Marie Geoffroy and Mahault Albacarrin, *Mémoires et thèses reliés à la diversité sexuelle et la pluralité des genres parus au Québec de 2000 à 2014*, 5.

59 The documents contain terms like trans, transgender, genderqueer, etc. in their titles.

> We must insist on the importance of integrating trans people into LGBT research teams […].[60]

Though I cannot help but agree with the above statement, it nevertheless comes from research teams composed primarily of self-identified cis people, that which do not include trans* people as co-researchers or professors, but rather include them as assistant researchers (which is a start). As activists and researchers Viviane Namaste, Nora Butler Burke, and Zack Marshall demonstrate, it is essential that we take a closer look at *how* and *why* trans* people are included in research projects:

> Rather than simply celebrating attention to trans people by a national AIDS organization, [our] letter inquires as to how and why 'trans people' have emerged as a new category within public health, including the access to grants (often by non-trans people) implicit therein.[61]

To make use of a culinary analogy, to "add and mix" is not enough, because the addition of ingredients, their quantities, techniques, and the timing of these additions will alter a recipe. Denouncing the fact that all too often, research projects led by cis people consult with trans* people during or at the end of the research process, Namaste, Burke, and Marshall insist that trans* people need to be actively included during *all* stages of the research process. I would add that they must also actively hold some of the most *fundamental roles* of these projects. Power is not distributed evenly across all members of a research team. According to funding agencies, research teams are divided into the following roles, from the most important (those with the greatest decision-making, administrative, and financial power) to the least important: principal investigators, co-investigators (active participants in the decision-making process), collaborator(s) (similar to co-investigators, but not necessarily affiliated with an academic institution), partner organizations, and

60 Enriquez, et al., "Développer les études trans dans la francophonie," 100.

61 Namaste, *et al.* "Critiquing the AIDS Bureaucracy: An Open Letter to the Canadian AIDS Society," in *Oversight: Critical Reflections on Feminist Research and Politics*, ed. Vivian Namaste (Toronto: Women's Press, 2015), 109.

research assistants. While the inclusion of trans* people across all these roles is important, and while we can rejoice at the inclusion of trans* people in collaborator, partner organization, or research assistant roles, trans* people should also occupy more *central* positions, such as principal investigators or co-investigators. A well-known argument of feminist studies illustrates that, while we can celebrate the increased presence of women in the labour market, the fight for equality cannot stop there; the struggle for access to positions of power has been denounced as a barrier known as the glass ceiling. It is not insignificant that, like women, trans* people, though included in research projects, do not occupy positions of power. In other words, there exists a glass ceiling for trans* people in research projects conducted *on* trans* realities, which prevents them from accessing higher positions on research teams and in institutions. In a society in which trans* people experience significant economic and employment discrimination, as noted by Namaste, Burke, and Marshall, it is crucial that we shatter this glass ceiling: "Any work to be done ought to prioritize or at least seriously consider employing trans people, given the difficulties trans people have in employment […]."[62]

Namaste, Burke, and Marshall condemn the opportunism of certain groups working on topics concerning lesbians, gays, bisexuals, and HIV, who seek funding to include trans* people in their work without, however, being accountable towards them: "How exactly can national AIDS organizations obtain funding for work on trans people without demonstrating that there has been meaningful consultation with trans communities?"[63]

Their objective is not to criticize such groups per se, but to use this example to raise awareness about how research on trans* realities is conducted by cis people. In the same spirit, I would like to offer the example of "Knowledges on Inclusion and Exclusion of LGBTQ People (2016-23)," conducted as part of the (SSHRC) partnership grant program, which recently received 2.5 million dollars to address, among other things, the employment discrimi-

62 Ibid., 113.
63 Ibid., 118.

nation experienced by trans* people. Though we can celebrate this research team, (whose principal investigator, Line Chamberland, has worked tirelessly to integrate the concerns of trans* people in her work over the last few years), that includes 54 researchers and 48 partners, for having included some trans* people and several trans* organizations among its collaborators, the 21 university researchers from 14 universities[64] are not, to my knowledge, self-identified trans* people. How do we explain then, despite the great number of trans* people specializing in trans* issues and possessing the required qualifications to take part in this type of research, the absence of trans* scholars on this research team? This is just one example among many of the glass ceiling experienced by trans* people in academia. As previously mentioned, the aim is not to target any one team or institution—and in this case the team has made an effort to integrate trans* non-academics—rather, it is to question the general trend by which trans* experts are not generally integrated as co-investigators in funded research projects that deal with trans* issues.[65] This example illustrates how the question of the "T" in the LGBTQ acronym can sometimes be diluted.

As for the teaching of trans* issues in French Canada, the situation is just as concerning. I offer the three francophone Canadian universities with gender and feminist studies programs as examples. Geoffroy and Albarracin demonstrate that the university with the most submitted dissertations and theses linked to sexual and gender diversity since the year 2000 is UQAM.[66] For this rea-

64 Research Chair on homophobia, "Une importante subvention pour la recherche sur les minorités sexuelles et de genre," http://chairehomophobie.uqam.ca/nouvelles/392-une-importante-subvention-pour-une-recherchelgbtq.html, Retrieved March 13th, 2017; SSHRC (Social Science and Humanities Research Council), "Subventions de partenariat: Attributions du concours de novembre 2015," http://www.sshrc-crsh.gc.ca/results-resultats/recipientsrecipiendaires/2015/partnerships-partenariats-fra.aspx, Retrieved March 13th, 2017.

65 A research team that received a grant to study trans* youth and that included no trans* co-researchers recently invited me to join their team. This initiative that should inspire other research teams.

66 Marie Geoffroy and Mahault Albacarrin, *Mémoires et thèses reliés à la*

son, I spend more time here discussing this university. The feminist studies program at UQAM integrates courses on sexual and gender diversity through the course offerings of the department of sexology.[67] There are three courses relating to sexual and gender diversity: *Homosexuality and Society*, *Citizenship and Sexual Minorities*, and the *History of Sexual Identities in the Western World*.[68] Though these three courses may include trans* issues (I was not able to access their course outlines), none but the last reference gender identity or trans* issues in their sexual diversity focused descriptions. In February 2017, the department of sexology announced two new courses that include trans* issues, the *Epistemology and History of Ideas About Sexualitie*s and *Intersectionality and Sexualities*,[69] in addition to their pre-existing course: *Gender Disorder and Atypical Sexualities* (which has been called out by students for its problematic title). While we can applaud the department of sexology's initiative to put in place two new courses in which trans* issues are discussed, it is important to note that, since their conception, these courses have never been taught by a trans* person. Moreover, the recent employment of a professor of sexology specializing in trans* issues[70] who does not self-identify as trans* suggests that the two new

diversité sexuelle et la pluralité des genres parus au Québec de 2000 à 2014, 4-6.

67 Many courses offered by the Institute of Feminist studies and Research at UQAM refer to the notion of gender and gender identity, but not in the cis/trans* sense. Trans* issues are not mentioned in the majority of the titles and descriptions of offered courses in the three cycles, with the exception of the course *Littérature et identité sexuée* [Literature and Sexual Identity] about figures labeled "hermaphrodites," "androgynous," and about practices of "transvestism," and the course *Sexualité, genres, feminisms* [Sexuality, Genders, Feminisms] that includes trans* issues. The other courses that deal with them through the Départment de sexologie [Department of Sexology] are discussed in the text.

68 Research Chair on homophobia, "Cours offerts à l'UQAM," (2017), http://chairehomophobie.uqam.ca/enseignement/cours-offerts-a-l-uqam.html. Retrieved March 13th, 2017.

69 Research Chair on homophobia, "Info-mensuelle février 2017" (2017), http://chairehomophobie.uqam.ca/index.php?optioncom_acymailing andctrl=archiveandtask=viewandmailid=64andkey=vELKaOwFandsubid=16 8gI9wrsGpVRh16andtmpl=component. Retrieved on March 13th, 2017

70 UQAM (Université du Québec à Montréal). "Du sang neuf en sciences humaines : neuf nouveaux professeurs viennent grossir les rangs de la Fac-

courses are likely to continue to be taught by cis people. This problem, however, does not concern this department alone. A report presented by sociology students at UQAM demonstrates an under-representation or absence of texts assigned in their seminars written by marginalized authors (women, racialized, Indigenous, disabled, and trans* people). Though there is still a lot of work to be done with respect to many marginalized groups, the sociology department's graduate student feminist committee at UQAM notes that *gender identity is the only dimension that is completely absent in the course outlines of their 23 analyzed seminars*: "We found no required readings written by trans or non-binary people. We therefore identify a complete absence of trans and non-binary authors."[71]

Université Laval, which has announced the launch of L'Institut Femmes, Sociétés, Égalité et Équité (IFSEE), as well as a new "gender studies" program, offers a master's level microprogram. Of its thirteen courses, only one, *Sexual Diversity and Social Intervention*, mentions trans* issues[72] in its description. This course is taught by people who do not self-identify as trans. The new professor hired by Université Laval to teach the courses offered in this microprogram is a self-identified cis person. While we see a desire to include trans* issues in the university curricula and syllabuses, as exemplified by the intersex and trans* issues panel convened at Université Laval for the fifteenth edition in 2017 of "l'Université féministe d'été," there is little structural change in relation to the contents of offered courses and programs. The third example of a university offering feminist and gender studies is the Université de Montréal, whose "minor in feminist, gender, and sexualities stud-

ulté," 7 octobre 2016, https://www.actualites.uqam.ca/2016/faculte-sciences-humaines-accueille-nouveaux-professeur. Retrieved February 13th, 2017.

71 Comité féministe des deuxième et troisième cycles de sociologie de l'UQAM, Portrait des auteur-es en lectures obligatoires dans les cours aux 2e et 3e cycles du Département de sociologie de l'UQAM: Rapport présenté au Département de sociologie (Montréal: UQAM, 2017), 8.

72 Université Laval, "Microprogramme de deuxième cycle en études du genre" (2017), https://www.ulaval.ca/les etudes/ programmes/repertoire/details/microprogramme-de-deuxieme-cycle-en-etudes-du-genre.html#presentation-generale, Retrieved March 13th, 2017.

ies" has opened its doors to a first cohort in Fall 2017.[73] A systematic analysis of the titles and descriptions of the 30 courses offered in this new program reveals that, though many of them address sexual orientations and identities, none of them mention trans* issues. The university has not yet announced any new tenure-track positions in feminist and gender studies, but it is reasonable to assume that if none of its courses address trans* issues, the eventual opening of a position will not include a specialization in trans* studies. To make my argument clear: while we can rejoice over these developments in feminist and gender studies in French Canada, it appears that the concept of gender, as it is understood by these universities and departments, remains overwhelmingly cis-centred. My aim is to shed light on the cis-temic nature of often well-intentioned departments/programs, which perpetuate these problems unintentionally, allowing for cis people who specialize in trans* issues to be employed over trans* people. Consequently, at time of writing (in 2017), *in the history of francophone Canadian universities, no trans* person specializing in trans* issues has ever been employed in any department (my employment in 2018 would therefore be a first in Canadian history). Can we really go on claiming that these are simply coincidental departmental preferences? Isn't it time we address the structural forces that have created a glass ceiling for trans* people in universities and have directly and indirectly led to the total exclusion of trans* people among the francophone professors on a national scale?*

As explained by Marchand, Saint-Charles, and Corbeil, the glass ceiling phenomenon experienced by certain groups does not take place in a vacuum and is founded on existing (sexist, racist, cissexist, etc.) power relations that manifest themselves through a series of micro-aggressions that may initially seem trivial, such as those listed in this article, but are part of a global system and remain invisible: "The glass ceiling refers to these barriers or difficulties, at times barely perceptible, which impede ascending mo-

73 University of Montéal, "Mineure en études féministes, des genres et des sexualités" (2017), https://admission.umontreal.ca/programmes/mineure-en-etudes-feministes-des-genres-et-des-sexualites/structure-du-programme/, Retrieved April 13th, 2017.

bility […]."[74] If those trans* people specializing in trans* issues do not occupy professor positions in French Canada, it is not because of their absence, but because of the obstacles obstructing their "ascending mobility" in the world of academia. Trans* people are present in all other university positions (teaching assistants, limited-term appointment professors, research assistants, independent researchers, students) and perform a significant amount of often unpaid labour behind the scenes to help cis people pursue their interests in trans* issues. Over the past twelve months, at more than one university, I have, for example, led several workshops for university staff and faculty to raise awareness about trans* discrimination in university settings, sat on committees seeking to develop trans-inclusive policies, taught three-hour classes in the courses and seminars of professors hoping to integrate a session on trans* issues, acted as external reviewer of theses addressing trans* issues, co-supervised students Ph.D. theses, provided references and advice for multiple students working on trans* issues, reviewed several articles addressing trans* issues, and I have done a number of media interviews as an expert on trans* issues. None of this work was paid, as I had not yet been hired as a professor. Mine is not an isolated case; it represents the norm. As many trans* people have noted in their work,[75] in public discussion forums, in closed group forums (the Trans PhD Network Facebook page, for example), as well as in discussions during events such as the "Trans* Studies: An International Transdisciplinary Conference," which brought together almost 500 trans* studies researchers, this is a common occurrence. *One topic in particular, recurring like a leitmotiv in these discussions, is that people are confined to precarious employment positions in the university setting and yet are invited to perform unpaid, invisible labour furthering the careers of cis people.*

Does this phenomenon of unpaid and invisible labour not evoke the situation of women vis-à-vis men (and other minorities

74 Isabelle Marchand, *et al.*, "L'ascension professionnelle et le plafond de verre dans les entreprises privées au Québec," *Recherches féministes* 20, no. 1 (2007), 30.

75 Namaste, *et al*, "Critiquing the AIDS Bureaucracy."

vis-à-vis dominant groups)? Genuine allyship from professors and researchers in feminist and gender studies would consist of making visible the unpaid, invisible labour already performed by trans* people (from which these professors and researchers benefit), promoting the employment and inclusion of trans* people as co-investigators on their research teams, giving trans* people priority to teach courses on trans* issues, and thinking critically about their identities as cis people participating in research projects on trans* realities. In short, it is now time to move from education and research *about* trans* people to education and research *by/for* trans* people. The purpose of this critical analysis is not to discourage cis people from researching and/or teaching about trans* issues. On the contrary, such work is essential. Nevertheless, it is equally important that we invert the prevailing statistics, so that the majority of research and teaching positions concerning trans* issues are conducted and held by trans* people.

4. Transfeminism and the Subversion of Cisgender Identity

> This chapter seeks to name the violence of these occlusions, disavowals, and denials [of trans* people in Feminist studies] as part of a disciplinary but also historical and ideological imaginary. […] A transfeminist reconceptualization of women's studies seems vital.[76]

As suggested by this quote, the exclusion of trans* people from feminist and gender studies programs is not accidental, but rather an active part of the constitution of this field and its methodological approaches and epistemological frames, which are founded on cisgendernormativity. The invisible cisgender adjectives in gender analyses are at the heart of what has allowed this field to place

76 Noble, "Trans. Panic, Some Thoughts toward a Theory of Feminist Fundamentalism," 48.

trans* issues, realities, bodies, and identities exterior to feminist and gender studies. Seen from this angle the transfeminist approach has significant heuristic potential to subvert the ciscentred feminist subject. Transfeminism, which combines trans* and feminist approaches, was developed in the late 1990s and early 2000s by Anglophone theorists and activists such as Emi Koyama, who wrote the first *Transfeminist Manifesto*, Krista Scott-Dixon,[77] and Julia Serano.[78] On the francophone side, though the roots of a transfeminism can be unearthed in Bourcier and Espineira,[79] journalist Lalla Kowska-Régnier[80] seems to have been the first to use the term during a conference in 2005.[81] The first use of "transfeminism" as a term in francophone academic work can be found in my own texts[82], which recommend the adoption of this approach to analyze male privilege in trans* men. Recent developments in transfeminist approaches, such as Stryker, Currah, and Moore,[83] and Noble[84] most notably, invite us to conceive of transfeminism as not only a framework combining trans* and feminist analyses, but also as an approach that transcends "trans" as a term, going beyond sex and/or gender issues. Stryker, Currah, and Moore conceive

77 Krista Scott-Dixon, *Trans/Forming Feminisms.*

78 Serano, *Whipping Girl.*

79 See M.H./Sam Bourcier, "Des 'femmes travesties' aux pratiques transgenres"; —, *Sexpolitiques: Queer Zones* 2; —, *Queer Zones. Politique des identités sexuelles et des savoirs*. —, "Technotesto: biopolitiques des masculinités tr(s)ans hommes," —, *Queer Zones 3. Identités, cultures et politiques*; and Karine Espineira, *La transidentité. De l'espace médiatique à l'espace public*; —, "Pour une épistémologie trans et féministe"; —, *Transidentités: ordre et panique de genre*. See also Karine Espineira and M.H./Sam Bourcier, "Transfeminism: Something Else, Somewhere Else," *TSQ: Transgender Studies Quarterly* 3.1-2 (2016). They theorize the emergence of a transfeminist praxis in Europe between the years 1990-2000, even if the term "transfeminism" was not used.

80 Lalla Kowska-Régnier, "Trans féminisme ou Transinisme?"

81 Elsa Dorlin, *Sexe, genre et sexualités*, (Paris : Presses Universitaire de France, 2008). Dorlin briefly discusses the transfeminist praxis, but does not define and use the transfeminist approach.

82 Baril, "Transsexualité et privilèges masculins. Fiction ou realité?"

83 Stryker, Currah, Moore, "Introduction: Trans-, Trans, or Transgender?".

84 Noble, "Trans Panic."

of trans* analyses as having the potential to transgress multiple categories, whether theoretical, epistemological, or disciplinary, and propose the deployment of "trans," like that of "queer" as a verb, in new contexts: "those of us schooled in the humanities and social sciences have become familiar, over the past twenty years or so, with queering things; how might we likewise begin to critically trans- our world?"[85] Noble takes up this perspective when he writes of his desire to: "retrace the shape of women's studies by transing its epistemologies, disciplinarities, and methodologies."[86]

This is the lens through which I conclude this article. As I have demonstrated, while feminist and gender studies programs need to start decentring their cis-centred approaches, the problematic absence of trans* people with expertise in trans* issues in francophone universities, as well Canadian universities more generally, has cis-temic roots. The structural mechanisms that feed this cis-tem include disciplinary divisions, which I call disciplinary sectarianism:[87] each discipline protects its own territory, defends its own methodological approaches and theoretical frames, canonizes authors and establishes the limits of what counts as "real" philosophy, sociology, anthropology, sexology, etc., while concurrently relegating many researchers and students to the margins of the discipline. Those necessarily interdisciplinary people who work from anti-oppression and intersectional perspectives are therefore excluded from these fields, since their work is not perceived as fitting neatly into any of these disciplines. Extending beyond direct discrimination targeting their transness, trans* people specializing in trans* issues see themselves excluded from tenure-track positions because of indirect or invisible discrimination rooted, notably, in the idea that trans* issues do not belong in philosophy, sociology, or other disciplines. No department feels that such issues concern them, relegating them to other disciplines, along with the potential for new hires: the philosophy department stipulates that such issues are relevant to the social questions tackled in sociology, the sociol-

85 Stryker, Currah, Moore, "Introduction", 13.
86 Noble, "Trans. Panic." 47.
87 Ibid., 55. Here Noble speaks of "disciplinary fundamentalism."

ogy department considers these questions to be linked to feminist and gender studies, and feminist and gender studies believe trans* studies need to form their own autonomous discipline.

Social problems, including the oppression experienced by marginalized peoples such as trans* people, remain unintelligible thanks to such disciplinary sectarianisms. Though social problems are complex and stem from multiple, intertwined factors, as exemplified by intersectional feminist analyses, we must adopt multiple, complex, theoretical, epistemological, and methodological approaches that call for the *trans-cending* of disciplinary divisions. Like Roland Barthes, who asserts that interdisciplinarity,

> begins effectively (and not by the simple utterance of a pious hope) when the solidarity of the old disciplines breaks down—perhaps even violently, through the shocks of fashion to the advantage of a new object, a new language, neither of which is precisely this discomfort of classification which permits diagnosing a certain mutation…[88]

I believe that it is epistemologically and heuristically valuable to start a dialogue between disciplines in order to find solutions to the structural problems experienced by marginalized groups. Through this *trans-ing*, the transfeminist approach (as it is defined here), would allow for the transgression of the disciplinary sectarianism that prevents trans* people from fully participating in the academic sphere. Although it is appropriate for feminist and gender studies to question their cisgendernormativity, the invitation introduced here targets all disciplines. After all, could the "renewal of feminism in francophone philosophy" not go through a *trans-ing* that would allow for the breakdown of disciplinary barriers between feminist studies and philosophy, between feminist and trans* studies, and between philosophy and trans* studies?

88 Roland Barthes, *The Rustle of Language*, trans. Richard Howard (California: University of California Press, 1989), 56.

WAYS OF BEING IN THE ALL-TOO-PRESENT BODY

Attending to and through Chronic Pain

A. REBECCA ROZELLE-STONE

I must let this pain flow through me and pass on. If I resist or try to stop it, it will detonate inside me, shatter me, splatter my pieces against every wall and person that I touch.

—Audre Lorde[1]

In her book, *The Rejected Body*, Susan Wendell warns against both simplistic imperatives of "mind over body" with their attendant "myths of control"[2] in cases of illness and disability as well as uncritical celebrations of philosophies of the body that involve the wholesale rejection of mind-body dualism. While many feminists[3] have understandably decried perspectives and practices that promote "bare perceptual cognition" and a sense of self over and against an unintelligent body, Wendell, who has lived with Myalgic Encephalomyelitis (M.E.)—or what has formerly been referred

1 Audre Lorde, *The Cancer Journals* (San Francisco: Aunt Lute Books, 1997), 10.

2 Susan Wendell, *The Rejected Body* (New York: Routledge, 1996), 98.

3 Notably: Simone de Beauvoir, *The Second* Sex, ed. and trans. Constance Borde and Sheila Malovany-Chevallier (New York: Vintage Books, 2011); Elizabeth Spelman in "Woman as Body: Ancient and Contemporary Views," *Feminist Studies* 8 (1): 109-31, Spring 1982; and Susan Bordo, *Unbearable Weight: Feminism, Western Culture, and the Body*, 10th Anniversary Edition (Berkeley: University of California Press, 2004).

to as Chronic Fatigue Syndrome (C.F.S.)—since 1985 and is still intermittently impaired by "fatigue, muscle pain, muscle weakness, dizziness, nausea, headaches, depression, and problems with short-term memory (especially verbal recall),"[4] makes a strong case that the easy rejection of mind-body dualism (and of what she calls "transcendence of the body"[5]) may itself stem from a privileged position. That is, healthy subjects who are generally unfamiliar with the experiences of chronic suffering or debilitating disease will tend to overlook the value of "some emotional and cognitive distance from"[6] bodily experiences that are unpredictable, unreliable, painful, chaotic, and sometimes even paralyzing. Unfortunately, in her view, feminist theory has not fully confronted and articulated a phenomenology of bodily suffering, and therefore it "has not taken account of a very strong reason for wanting to transcend the body."[7]

Nevertheless, Wendell points out, strategies of bodily transcendence that expand possibilities of experience beyond the body's sufferings do not necessarily signify devaluation or neglect of that body. Drawing on Drew Leder's phenomenological insights from *The Absent Body*, she recognizes that in fact, the "onset of illness, disability, or pain destroys the 'absence' of the body to consciousness...and forces us to find conscious responses to new, often acute, awareness of our bodies." Thus, she continues, "the body itself takes us into and then beyond its sufferings and limitations."[8] So while pain makes the body "present" to us, often with an insistence that absorbs our full attention, the suffering body need not have the last word or serve as the locus for ultimate meaning. In short, Wendell introduces greater ambivalence in theories about the relationship of consciousness to bodies by taking seriously the complex experiences of chronic pain sufferers like herself; her in-

4 Susan Wendell, "Unhealthy Disabled: Treating Chronic Illnesses as Disabilities," *Hypatia* 16.4 (2001) 2, 32.

5 Wendell, *The Rejected Body*, 177.

6 Ibid., 178.

7 Ibid., 169.

8 Ibid., 178.

terest is in "strategies of daily living, not grand spiritual victories,"[9] in the context of the crises of meaning brought on by the pain. She writes, "I do not think that we need to subscribe to some kind of mind-body dualism to recognize that there are degrees to which consciousness and the sense of self may be tied to bodily sensations and limitations, or to see the value of practices…that loosen the connection."[10] We are left to ask: *Is it not altogether reasonable, in such a context, to attempt to disengage from certain constrictive bodily sensations and moods by creatively redirecting consciousness, by taking on an "observer's attitude,"*[11] *so that the pained body does not dictate the totality of the sufferer's experience?*

Wendell's insights about how chronic illness affects the ways and the values of attending to her body have some fecund if unexpected intersections with the ideas and experiences of the French philosopher, Christian mystic, and social activist Simone Weil (1909-1943), an oft-neglected interlocutor, especially in contemporary feminist-disability studies conversations.[12] In part, this neglect is likely explained by the well-known influence of Platonic philosophy on her thought—the very tradition that is the source of deep historical devaluations of the body (especially women's bodies) and of somatic experience in general. Moreover, as Wendell points out, "Feminists have also argued that the dominant forms of Christian theology strengthened these ancient views by representing the body as a major source of the desires and weaknesses that lead to sin, and overcoming the body as an essential ingredient in moral perfection."[13] But Weil's thought—though often simplistically characterized as "Christian Platonic"—is, as I will show, not so easy to categorize and does not neatly fall under an orthodox

9 Ibid., 177.
10 Ibid., 178.
11 Ibid., 174.
12 I wish to extend gratitude to the anonymous reviewer of this article, who suggested that it is positioned between the fields of disability studies, critical phenomenology, and feminist philosophies. Indeed, it was my aim to bring these fields into conversation with each other, especially as they converge at times with Simone Weil's insights on suffering, without conflating any of them.
13 Wendell, *The Rejected Body*, 165.

"Christian" (or even Platonic) rubric. There is abundant evidence, for instance, that Weil is not only *not* anti-body, but that she takes experiences of suffering and affliction quite seriously, and in ways that address the failures that Wendell finds in contemporary feminist theories of the body.

In her later essays and notebooks, Weil wrote extensively about the relationship between suffering and a certain kind of attention. She would agree, for instance, with Wendell when the latter says that "living with pain, fatigue, nausea, unpredictable abilities, and/or the imminent threat of death creates different *ways of being* that give valuable perspectives on life and the world. Thus, although most of us want to avoid suffering if possible, suffering is part of some valuable ways of being."[14] Central to these "valuable ways of being," for Weil, is the development of a kind of attention capable of disrupting parochial and self-centered perspective and facilitating an *impersonal* recognition of others' sufferings and trials. That is, pain—especially the experience of chronic pain or long-term illness—when undergone by a subject who refuses to supplement a *referential object* for the pain, makes possible compassionate attention to and communion with the world that is largely inaccessible to those whose bodies are regularly pain-free and thus experientially "absent." Further, Weil describes the possibility of a radical shift in the nature and focus of attention in some cases of long-suffering: while attention is initially directed to one's (personal, bodily) pain to seek out relief in a pragmatic fashion, it can, with a certain kind of consent to the suffering,[15] become wholly disposed toward concerns and injustices that extend beyond one's

14 Susan Wendell, "Unhealthy Disabled: Treating Chronic Illnesses as Disabilities," 31.

15 I draw on and will explain Simone Weil's notion of "consent" in Section II of this paper, "Attending to Impersonal Pain: Feeling the Universe." Yet Susan Wendell describes a decision in her own suffering that is similar to Weil's consent. Wendell writes: "With chronic pain, I must remind myself over and over again that the pain is meaningless, that there is nothing to fear or resist, that resistance only creates tension, which makes it worse. When I simply notice and *accept the pain*, my mind is often freed to pay attention to something else. This is not the same as ignoring my body, which would be dangerous…" Wendell, *The Rejected Body*, 173.

personal interests. However, this "impersonal" attention is founded on and never "forgets" the particular body in pain; the particular suffering body serves as a link to the reality of the universe and of our own mortality, the realization of which can break through our egocentrism. As Weil herself writes, "To change the relationship between ourselves and the world in the same way as, through apprenticeship, the workman changes the relationship between himself and the tool. Getting hurt: this is the trade entering into the body. May all suffering make the universe enter into the body."[16]

To explain this *in-corporation* of the world undergone via pain, this essay proceeds in two sections. In this first section, I examine some influential phenomenological descriptions of the body[17] in pain, noting the initial direction and function of attention in this context. Drawing primarily on Drew Leder's and Elaine Scarry's works, we find helpful meditations on the minute affects and tendencies undergone when we are in pain. In the second section, I proffer an analysis of the transformation from those "personal" responses to "impersonal" attention by looking closely at Weil's descriptions of affliction, consent to suffering, impersonality, and the corresponding (ethical) attention that, in her thought, displaces the faculty of imagination. While Weil might be said ultimately to argue for a transcendence of the *ego* rather than, as Wendell proposed, a transcendence of the body, her model of attention underscores the importance of the perspective gained by consenting to—rather than detaching from—ongoing pain. Moreover, Weil is critical of those who would romanticize affliction or suggest in any

16 Simone Weil, *Gravity and Grace*, trans. Emma Crawford and Mario von der Ruhr (New York: Routledge, 2004), 141.

17 Wendell, *The Rejected Body*, 194. Of course Susan Wendell is right to cite Adrienne Rich who wrote: "Perhaps we need a moratorium on saying 'the body'…When I write 'the body,' I see nothing in particular. To write 'my body' plunges me into lived experience, particularity…" Adrienne Rich, "Notes for a Politics of Location" *Blood, Bread, and Poetry: Selected Prose 1979-1985*, (New York: Norton, 1986), 215. I find myself in a similar position as Wendell, however, in resorting to the term "the body," since so much has already been written in this framework, and moreover, in my arguing for the cultivation of *impersonal* attention, discussion of "the body" comes to acquire a significance for which "my body" is insufficient.

way that it has some ultimate *telos*, but she does describe the unique recognitions and capabilities that are founded in chronic pain. To say, descriptively, that chronic pain affords me a particular insight is not to say, prescriptively, that I ought to seek out (if that were even possible) chronic pain as a means of attaining some valorized standard of action or attitude.

Rather, as we strive to learn from the multifarious sufferings of others, we must attempt to understand possibilities (and real instances) of connection and communion in situations that ordinarily constrain, alienate, limit, and even paralyze us. What sort of knowledge is lost when we ignore or avoid the experiences of long-term sufferings of others (or ourselves)? Wendell describes this epistemic significance:

> It is difficult for most people who have not lived with prolonged or recurring pain to understand the benefits of accepting it. Yet some people who live with chronic pain speak of 'making friends' with it as the road to feeling better and enjoying life. How do they picture their pain and think about it; what kind of attention do they give it and when; how do they live around and through it, and what do they learn from it? We could all learn this as part of our education.... People with painful disabilities can teach us about pain, because they cannot avoid it and have had to learn how to face it and live with it.[18]

What, indeed, will these lessons entail, and what could they mean for the person who doesn't (yet) experience the constrictions of chronic pain? How might this pathic knowledge realign our attitudes towards our own and others' bodies?

I. Attending to Personal Pain: Healing My Body

Phenomenologies of pain (such as those articulated by Elaine Scarry and Drew Leder) are of course indebted to Maurice Merleau-Ponty's works for their incisive descriptions of the lived body,

18 Wendell, *The Rejected Body*, 109.

its self-effacing tendencies in everyday sensing and functioning in the world, and its "presencing" tendencies in response to pain. In order to underscore the "weightiness"[19] of the phenomenon of chronic pain on the lived body and the corresponding effects on attention, I will review five characteristics of chronic pain that merit our reflection for the purposes of this essay. Here, it is important to qualify what is meant by "chronic pain," which is of course only one type of pain, but is the one that serves as the focus of this essay. Susan Wendell defines "chronic pain" as "pain that is not endured for some purpose or goal (unlike the pain of intense athletic training, for instance), pain that promises to go on indefinitely (although sometimes intermittently and sometimes unpredictably), pain that demands no action because as far as we know, no action can get rid of it."[20]

The first and most central characteristic is that there is *sensory intensification* brought on by pain, in which the affected area of the body seizes our attention, bringing what was background and eclipsed into the foreground. This is true not only of chronic pain, but also of acute and momentary pain, though some adaptability here is possible. As Drew Leder explains, "A chronic pain for which one has no solution continues to grab the attention with undiminished intensity…It is as if the pain were ever born anew, although nothing whatsoever has changed."[21] In general, aversive states bring us to a corporeal awareness; the affected part of the body is suddenly and insistently *present* to our consciousness. But pathology or injury is not necessary to bring about this sort of appearance. Leder notes, "When normal physiology reaches certain functional limits it seizes our attention. We remember the body at times of hunger, thirst, strong excretory needs, and the like. It is biologically adaptive that we recall our situation at such moments and that their unpleasantness exert a telic demand for removal."[22]

19 As Susan Wendell explains, "A body experienced has both limitations and weight." *The Rejected Body*, 168.

20 Ibid., 171.

21 Drew Leder, *The Absent Body* (Chicago: University of Chicago Press, 1990), 72-73.

22 Ibid., 84.

There is, then, biological utility for these nuisances; we are compelled to act to resolve the discomfort for however long the disruptive stimulus persists, even though we may be intellectually aware that no particular action (in the case of chronic pain) could relieve the distress.

This *imperative of action*, then, constitutes the second trait, although in the case of chronic pain, this imperative can be experienced as futile. Leder describes an "affective call" that pain sends to the subject, where this call "has a quality of compulsion."[23] As Elaine Scarry explains in *The Body in Pain*, pain (in general) is defined by being:

> a pure physical experience of negation, an immediate sensory rendering of "against," of something being against one, and of something one must be against. Even though it occurs within oneself, it is at once identified as "not oneself," "not me," as something so alien that it must right now be gotten rid of.[24]

The fact that pain is generally experienced as repulsive to us means that we wish to enact some change that will lessen the suffering, even if that change be merely a perspectival shift. With the onset of pain, we become pragmatically oriented, in an urgent kind of way that does not manifest when our bodies are comfortable. Our attention is initially seized by the pain and is also, therefore, of a pragmatic kind, concerned foremost with accomplishing tasks to the end of enabling biological survival. Leder writes,

> My own body becomes the object not just of perception and interpretation but of action. I seek medication, physical therapies, whatever will help. My projects are reorganized around the attempt to cope with or remove the pain. Instead of just acting *from* the body, I act *toward* it.[25]

Thus the imperative for action is *personally* framed; the sole objective is to *heal my body*. My focus, especially as a chronically ill

23 Ibid., 73.

24 Elaine Scarry, *The Body in Pain* (New York: Oxford University Press, 1985), 52.

25 Leder, *The Absent Body*, 79.

person, is (at least initially) turned inward, upon the minutiae of my bodily struggles. As Leder reminds us, "The consequent self-preoccupation of the ill is a well-recognized phenomenon. The… meticulous attention to the least bodily functions, the careful consideration of all acts as to their harmful or therapeutic effects, has both its tragic and comic aspects."[26]

The recent documentary film *Unrest*,[27] which is produced, directed by, and about Jennifer Brea and her experiences with M.E./C.F.S., reveals Brea's many desperate and sometimes comically absurd strategies, tactics, and home remedy "cures" (which included ingesting various supplements, meditation, avoidance all possibility of contact with mold which required her inhabiting a tent outside their home and instructing her husband to change clothes before entering the tent to avoid contamination, and fecal transplants) to mitigate the symptoms of M.E. after she was diagnosed in 2011. Though these attempts were portrayed by Brea herself as humorous in a certain light, the extreme attention to techniques of mastering her unpredictable symptoms also carried a sense of obsessive urgency. In light of the two aforementioned traits, then, we see that pain effectively withdraws our attention from the public world to the privacy of the body in an insistent way, but compels us to find resources—whether external or internal—to address the aversion of pain.

The third characteristic of pain highlights its *isolating nature*. As Leder describes it, "Pain exerts a phenomenologically 'centripetal' force, gathering space and time inward to the center. We are ceaselessly reminded of the here-and-now body."[28] While pleasure and happiness are naturally "expansive," opening us to more connections with the wider world,[29] there is a spatiotemporal constric-

26 Ibid., 81-82.

27 Jennifer Brea, *Unrest*, Film, (Los Angeles: Shella Films, 2017).

28 Ibid., 76.

29 This idea of pleasure having an expansive quality that enables us to forge connections in the world is tied to the Freudian concept of the "sexual instinct" or the life/erotic drive, which is a "constructive or assimilatory" process (Sigmund Freud, "Beyond the Pleasure Principle," *The Freud Reader*, ed. Peter Gay. [New York: W.W. Norton and Company, 1989], 618).

tion that accompanies the experience of intense pain; one feels nailed to the spot in the most extreme cases, and unable to think easily beyond the immediate physical crisis. Again, Leder affirms that this feature is true even of chronic pain: "While the body in well-being can explore the far reaches of time through memory and imagination, such possibilities constrict when we are in pain. With chronic suffering a painless past is all but forgotten."[30] There is, however, a paradox underlying the isolating and constricting experience of pain that Scarry explains as stemming from the "dissolution of the boundary between inside and outside," or "an almost obscene conflation of private and public." In the experience of physical pain, she tells us, there is "all the solitude of absolute privacy with none of its safety, all the self-exposure of the utterly public with none of its possibility for camaraderie or shared experience."[31] There is, at one and the same time, isolation and exposed vulnerability (although I will argue the isolation can be offset by the shared realizations acquired through pain).

Moreover, just as there exists a centripetal tendency in pain, there also exists a "*centrifugal movement*"[32] in which we precisely attempt to escape our pain and find reprieve by reaching outward into the world, or by trying to live in an idealized past, or by fleeing to an imagined future or state of being. We may identify this centrifugal movement as signaling the fourth noteworthy characteristic of pain, although technically the movement is a *response* to pain. The distinguishing feature relevant here is the "objectlessness" of chronic (or any) pain that provokes the hunt for an object. Scarry remarks that "physical pain is exceptional in the whole fabric of psychic, somatic, and perceptual states for being the only one that has no object."[33] While our sensual capacities like sight, hearing, touch, desire, and hunger have corresponding objects beyond the boundaries of the body—they are *intentional*—pain is characterized by a "complete absence of referential content."[34] Pain, Scarry ob-

30 Leder, *The Absent Body*, 76.
31 Scarry, *The Body in Pain*, 53.
32 Leder, *The Absent Body*, 76.
33 Scarry, *The Body in Pain*, 161.
34 Ibid., 162.

serves, "is not 'of' or 'for' anything—it is itself alone."[35] These other sensual capacities and states, precisely by taking objects, invite us to enter the natural, external world. (However, she also recognizes that "the more a habitual form of perception is experienced as itself rather than its external object, the closer it lies to pain."[36] For instance, if I am experiencing, self-consciously, *my seeing and its bodily locus*, rather than being taken up by the objects of my sight, I am moving toward the vicinity of painful awareness of my body. The images of objects meanwhile serve to displace the "weightiness" of my body and of my eyes in particular.)

But a state with no corresponding object (like pain) invites a supplementation—a need to *invent* a world or an object—especially when there are no obvious, immediate, and accessible remedies to diminish the objectless state. Pain festers; it creates a void. It is here that the imagination often enters the scene as the facilitator and inventor of objects. Scarry writes:

> Imagining is, in effect, the ground of last resort. That is, should it happen that the world fails to provide an object, the imagination is there, almost on an emergency stand-by basis, as a last resource for the generation of objects. Missing, they will be made-up; and though they may sometimes be inferior to naturally occurring objects, they will always be superior to naturally occurring objectlessness.[37]

Importantly, too, when sensual states and capacities (like hunger or desire) are for too long deprived of an object, they begin to approach the state of pain. Thus, Scarry later offers an example of the (psychic) pain of loneliness (unfulfilled desire for companionship): "Imagining a companion if the world provides none, may—at least temporarily—prevent longing from being a wholly self-experiencing set of physical and emotional events that, emptied of any referential content, exist as merely painful inner disturbances."[38] Imagination, then, as the centrifugal movement

35 Ibid.
36 Ibid., 165.
37 Ibid., 166.
38 Ibid., 167.

countering the centripetal force of pain, provides objects that may include: spiritual accolades, companions, gratitude from others, meanings, purposes, and a happier future, to eliminate as much as possible the pointless void that we experience as pain. Included here, I argue, are some of the "strategies of disengagement" that provided relief to Wendell.[39]

Corresponding to the objectless state of pain with its absence of referential content is the final characteristic: *silence*. That is, pain is either inarticulate (in the sense that its "privacy" and "objectlessness" renders it nearly impossible to be verbally objectified and communicated), or it silences all else. With regard to the latter aspect, the moment that pain can be accurately conveyed, rising strangely and horrifyingly out of the privacy of the sufferer's body, "it makes all further statements and interpretations seem ludicrous and inappropriate, as hollow as the world content that disappears in the head of the person suffering."[40] Not surprisingly, however, although such visceral expressions show the trivial nature of other speeches, the cries and other expressions of pain are quickly isolated and ignored—or else "explained" from a presumably more sophisticated perspective, whether philosophical, scientific, or religious, and thus are neutralized.[41]

39 For instance, Wendell writes, "Even being able to say, 'My brain is badly affected right now, so I am depressed, but I am fine and my life is going well,' is a way of asserting that the quality of my life is not completely dependent on the state of my body, that projects *can still be imagined* and accomplished, and *that the present is not all there is*." Emphases mine. (*The Rejected Body*, 174.)

40 Ibid., 60.

41 Sunaura Taylor describes this violent "neutralization" of the expressions of pain and fear in the experiences of animals about to be slaughtered. While there is a popular narrative of animals' supposed "voicelessness," Taylor makes clear that such is not the case: animals, like marginalized peoples, are (in the words of Arundhati Roy) the "preferably unheard." Describing a 2009 viral video in which a cow awaiting slaughter shows many explicit signs of fear, distress, anxiety, and panic, Taylor then comments: "I cannot read this animal's actions as anything other than the expression of fear and a desire not to be in that situation. There is no doubt: if she could tell us what she wanted it would be to turn around and leave that tunnel. We are choosing not to hear her" (Sunaura Taylor, *Beasts of Burden: Animal and Disability Liberation* [New

Of course it is often the case that inexpressible pain *also* silences all else. Dr. Stephen Grosz, a practicing psychoanalyst, recalls sessions with a 29-year old patient, "Anthony," who learned in the course of treatment that he was HIV positive. In the immediate weeks following the test results, Anthony described many disturbing dreams to his analyst. But Grosz observed that while "Anthony continued to speak about his life and feelings…his flow of words became slower and slower, until one day he became altogether silent."[42] Grosz reports that some days, in fact, "[Anthony] might lie down and be silent for the entire fifty minutes."[43] Realizing that his attempts to provoke Anthony to speak were often counter-productive and unnatural in the circumstances, Grosz himself was pulled into silence.

So now, given these five aspects of chronic pain—(1) the sensory intensification, (2) the affective call for remedial action, (3) the spatiotemporal constriction of attention, (4) the objectlessness with its centrifugal tendencies, and (5) the silence—we return to our original question: How might this knowledge deriving from experiences of ongoing pain realign our attitudes towards our own and others' bodies? Further, could there be a *development* of attention toward the external world, people, and other projects from an apparently *constricting* state? After all, Scarry tells us: "It is only when the body is comfortable, when it has ceased to be an obsessive object of perception and concern, that consciousness develops other objects, that for any individual the external world (in part already existing and in part about to be formed) comes into being and begins to grow."[44] Is she right about this?

York: The New Press, 2017], 67).

42 Stephen Grosz, *The Examined Life* (New York: W.W. Norton and Company, 2013), 200.

43 Ibid.

44 Elaine Scarry, *The Body in Pain*, 39.

II. Attending to and through Impersonal Pain: Feeling the Universe

Drew Leder, towards the end of *The Absent Body*, describes moral, aesthetic, and spiritual modalities that are manifestations of what he calls (utilizing a concept taken from Neo-Confucianism) "forming one body with the universe": compassion representing the moral sphere, absorption figuring the aesthetic sphere, and communion signifying the spiritual sphere.[45] While these modes represent possibilities for various forms of expansion via a realization of the transpersonal nature of the lived body, they do not answer the question of how the suffering individual's attention may ever shift away from a personal, utility-centered orientation. Simone Weil, too, was intent upon finding a way to expand her sensibilities into the entire universe, "of realizing the body that excludes nothing and reveals everything of moral and spiritual importance."[46] In her writings, we find explicit admonishment of those who would seek to deflect suffering through the object-providing imagination, and admiration for those who, by refusing consolations, consent to the objectless "void" of pain. These decrees are understandably controversial, but require some contextualization. In this final section, I undertake to explain the basis for these judgments and to show how consenting to the experience of chronic pain opens a new (impersonal) mode of being-in-the-world that could be characterized as ethically attentive.

First, it is important to point out that Susan Wendell actually recognized a "paradox" of chronic pain in her account of it, consisting in the fact that "a major aspect of the painfulness of pain [or the suffering caused by pain]...is the desire to get rid of it, to escape from it, to make it stop."[47] She thus recommended a kind of "acceptance toward it, giving in to it," or "making friends with" the pain that involved being aware of the pain, not resisting

45 See Drew Leder, *The Absent Body*, Chapter 6.

46 Ann Pirruccello, "Making the World My Body: Simone Weil and Somatic Practice," *Philosophy East and West*. 52 (4): 479-498, October 2002.

47 Wendell, *The Rejected Body*, 171.

it, but "relax[ing] 'into it.'"[48] In this way, she affirmed that pain for her was "no longer the phenomenon described by Leder" because she had transformed it into something that could hardly be experienced as aversive and would likely not be accompanied by the aforementioned traits.[49]

Simone Weil, too, recognized that pain is an interpreted experience, capable of transmutation. For instance, she wrote, "Pain is the color of certain events. When a man who can and a man who cannot read look at a sentence written in red ink, they both see the same red color, but this color is not so important for the one as for the other."[50] The one for whom the red color (pain) is less significant is the one who has gone through an "apprenticeship" in attention. Erazim Kohák, decades after Weil's death, made a similar remark in relation to the sense of pain experienced by one who conceives herself, amongst her modern conveniences and artifacts, the center of the universe, versus the sense of pain experienced by one who lives closely, intimately, and attentively with the land:

> Many of the injuries which keep urban emergency rooms busy warrant no more than a kerchief pressed to the wound and a wave of the hand. It is not that pain hurts less here [living close to the land]...The pain simply *matters less*. There is so much more that matters. When humans no longer think themselves the measure of all things, their pain is no longer a cosmic catastrophe. It becomes a part of a greater whole.[51]

Still, Weil did not place primacy on consenting to pain for pragmatic reasons such as the avoidance of real suffering (as we see in Wendell's account), nor did she take a teleological approach toward inevitable suffering (like seeing it as a "gift," as in Kohák's account). She said, for instance, "I should not love my suffering because it is useful. I should love it because it is," that is, because

48 Ibid.

49 Ibid.

50 Weil, *Waiting for God*, trans. Emma Craufurd (New York: Perennial Classics, 2001), 78.

51 Erazim Kohák, *The Embers and the Stars: A Philosophical Inquiry into the Moral Sense of Nature* (Chicago: University of Chicago Press, 1984), 43.

it is a real and inherent part of our being-in-the-world.[52] That one should not esteem *one's own* pain and suffering for the virtues it may produce does not, however, preclude recognizing a "value of suffering" itself, as when she wrote, "I believe in the value of suffering, so long as one makes every [legitimate] effort to escape it."[53]

Naturally, the question begged here is: What constitutes an *illegitimate* effort to escape suffering? Why should any attempt to avoid suffering, for instance in the case of chronic pain, be castigated? While Weil's conception of affliction [*malheur*] (of which prolonged pain is one variety[54]) reflects many of the aforementioned characteristics ascribed to pain—that it pins us to the present, that it has a silencing effect, and that it is an objectless state—she strongly repudiates the "centrifugal" tendencies supplied by the imagination to avoid the suffering of pain, even though she accepts that those tendencies are real and natural. In her *Cahiers*, she compares the workings of the imagination in contexts of suffering to forces of gravity [*pesanteur*]. At first glance, this is a strange comparison since the imaginative forays relieve the sufferer of the *weightiness* of the pain; contrary to the effect of gravity, the imagination appears to "lighten the load," hence its attraction. But for Weil, these centrifugal tendencies are gravitational because they reveal human *baseness* and mediocrity, like the tendency toward self-deception and illusion. She writes, "The imagination, filler up of the void, is essentially a liar."[55] That is, when we imagine a pleasant future so as to displace the present brutal reality, or when

52 Weil, *Gravity and Grace*, 80.

53 Weil, *First and Last Notebooks* (New York: Oxford University Press, 1970), 3. To be fair, Kohák also argues: "Alleviation must be the first answer to pain." Though he continues by insisting there are crucial questions we must ask alongside alleviation of pain: "Is the relief, good in itself, worth the price it would demand? Is the comfort of the drug worth the loss of sensitivity it exacts?" (*The Embers and the Stars*, 42, 43).

54 Weil, *Waiting for God*, 68. For Weil, *malheur* is no mere "attack of pain;" rather, as she says, "[t]here is not real affliction unless the event that has seized and uprooted a life attacks it, directly or indirectly, in all its parts, social, psychological, and physical. The social factor is essential. There is not really affliction [*malheur*] unless there is social degradation or the fear of it in some form or another" (*Waiting for God*, 68).

55 Weil, *Gravity and Grace*, 16.

the religious devotee imagines "a God who smiles on [him]"[56] to compensate for his meaningless trials, or when the lonely person imagines the perfect companion to supplant her complicated (or absent) partner, then we trigger disconnections founded on our myopic interests and are guilty of an ersatz attention. Rather than being receptive to the givenness of the world as it really stands, in our efforts to flee certain forms of suffering, we distort, project, and fabricate others as dictated by our egoistic desires.

We should not mistake Weil as saying that pain should always go unrelieved, that comfort should not be provided, or that affliction and suffering should not be prevented.[57] To the contrary, she thinks that we are under strict obligation to attend to and respond directly to the needs of all humans, but most urgently to those who are unjustly suffering. However, we are limited in our abilities to provide assistance—whether to ourselves or to others—and for Weil it is paramount that we respect the limits of the real and resist fantasy, projection, and escapism, for this resistance is the cornerstone of what it is to be attentive (and thus to be loving and ethical in her account). Moreover, our "centrifugal tendencies" not only prevent us from appropriately responding to our own and others' real needs, but also constitute forms of violence themselves. Reflecting on her own chronic migraines, she writes,

> I must not forget that at certain times when my headaches were raging I had an intense longing to make another human being suffer by hitting him in exactly the same part of his forehead... When in this state, I have several times succumbed to the temptation at least to say words which cause pain. Obedience to the force of gravity. The greatest sin.[58]

56 Ibid., 9.

57 For instance, she writes: "We have to say like Ivan Karamazov that nothing can make up for a single tear from a single child, and yet to accept all tears and the nameless horrors which are beyond tears. We have to accept these things, not in so far as they bring compensations with them, but in themselves. We have to accept the fact that they exist simply because they do exist"; and "we should make every effort we can to avoid affliction, so that the affliction which we meet with may be perfectly pure and perfectly bitter," *Gravity and Grace*, 80-1.

58 Ibid., 2-3.

Or again: "Headaches. At a certain moment, the pain is lessened by projecting it into the universe, but the universe is impaired."[59] Even our deflections of suffering and our fabricated consolations, as benign as they may appear, problematically function to preserve our (imagined) centeredness in the world, at the expense of everyone and everything else. The challenge is to abandon a purely personal perspective in favor of an impersonal (possibly animal?[60]) one that would enable us to see our *relative position* in the grand scheme of things.

Still, Weil makes stark pronouncements about affliction and suffering that are prima facie radically insensitive. Were it not for the authority she claims by her own well-known physical sufferings, including these frequent and near-paralyzing migraines, and the consistency of her life with her ideas, we might be justified in dismissing her as yet another privileged moralist. It was not, then, from abstract principle that she wrote, on May 12, 1942, to a permanently paralyzed soldier (Joë Bousquet) who had fought in World War I:

> I believe that the root of evil, in everybody perhaps, but certainly in those whom affliction has touched and above all if the affliction is biological, is day-dreaming. It is the sole consolation, the unique resource of the afflicted; the one solace to help them bear the fearful burden of time…So how could it be possible to renounce it? It has only one disadvantage, which is that it is unreal. To renounce it for the love of truth is really to abandon all one's possessions in a mad excess of love…[61]

She goes on to clarify that the problem with "day-dreaming" or

59 Ibid., 6-7.

60 While this subject would require its own separate treatment, I think there is good reason to reinterpret Weil's notion of the "impersonal" as something more affirmative—"animal." As Sunaura Taylor puts it, describing her disability as necessitating creative uses of her body, "I feel animal in my embodiment, and this feeling is one of connection, not shame. Recognizing my animality has in fact been a way of claiming the dignity in the way my body and other non-normative and vulnerable bodies move, look, and experience the world around them" (*Beasts of Burden*, 115).

61 Weil, *Seventy Letters* (New York: Oxford University Press, 1965), 139.

the imagination is that "it is falsehood. It excludes love. Love is real."[62] Love, then, for her is constituted by attention, and attention is a "watching, waiting" regard with no motive.[63] Weil explains that attention "consists of suspending our thought, leaving it detached, empty, and ready to be penetrated by the object" in its naked truth.[64] As Sharon Cameron has explained it, "Seeing like this—without identification—is seeing that resists 'reading.'"[65] Anat Pick develops this interpretation of Weil when she writes, "Attention is antiphilosophical; it does not produce arguments or truth claims about its object. Vulnerability as an object of attention does not yield a moral 'reading.'"[66] Yet the orientation of attention itself can be evaluated as moral insofar as it does *not* issue judgments or even reprieves. At the end of her letter to Bousquet, Weil asserts that love/attention is never a consolation, but "leaves pain completely intact."[67] How can this be, if love or ethical attention is to have any meaning for our embodied existence?

While Weil, I contend, did *not* mean that loving attention cannot offer up real, physical and/or psychical assistance—in fact, one of her frequently cited exemplars of attention is the image of the Good Samaritan—she *did* mean that the pain of our conscious mortality and its limitations cannot and should not be disguised. Unconsoled pain, in *this sense*, by precisely awakening us to the here-and-now, through the shock of its disruption to our own fantasies of limitlessness,[68] compels us to confront the finite, mortal, and precarious world in its vulnerability. As Pick explains, for Weil,

62 Ibid.

63 Weil, *Waiting for God*, 64.

64 Ibid., 62.

65 Sharon Cameron, *Impersonality* (Chicago: University of Chicago Press, 2007), 117.

66 Anat Pick, *Creaturely poetics: Animality and vulnerability in literature and film* (New York: Columbia University Press, 2011), 5.

67 Weil, *Seventy Letters*, 142.

68 For an extended discussion of Weil's conception and critique of these fantasies of limitlessness (or what she calls *l'imagination combleuse*) see A. Rebecca Rozelle-Stone and Lucian Stone's *Simone Weil and Theology* (New York: Bloomsbury, 2013), especially Chapter 3, "Human Nature and Decreation."

"Consolatory thinking (intellectual, psychological, or religious)… comes at the expense of appreciating reality and must therefore be overcome."[69] Wendell expresses a similar sentiment: "I regard the current level of cultural idealization, objectification, quest for perfection, and demand for control of the body as a collective sickness of the soul, an alienation from experience and reality."[70] Chronic pain, in this sense, is not only the root of an actively attentive disposition, but also of a new bodily knowledge stemming *from* attention that could neither be anticipated nor contrived from the standpoint of the healthy body that recedes from direct experience. Though pain would appear to constrict our human possibilities, the sufferer who "makes friends with" the fact of her pain has come into contact with a "necessity" that is uniquely educative and thus truly liberating. Cameron articulates this subtle point in Weil's philosophy well:

> One way to understand…attention is to see that Weil is not choosing servitude when she could be choosing freedom. Rather, she is seeing the difference between an imaginary freedom (the "I") and a necessary bondage to the real. Given such a construction, one couldn't have freedom simply by looking away from bondage. One could only have illusion. Thus attention frees one from imaginary confinement. But it simultaneously reveals the impossibility of being free from the conditions of the real. Attention does not then deceive one into equating the real with what is desirable.[71]

So while an experiential "absence" of my body (had usually in times of health and comfort) is undoubtedly desirable, I must admit the illusion that (subconsciously) accompanies that state of being: that I am indefatigable, invincible, even immortal. Pain serves to illuminate the reality of my materiality, vulnerability, and the fact of mortal limits, and in so doing, reminds me of my decentralized place in the suffering world at large. This awareness, along with the continual resistance to tempting falsehoods, is attention

69 Anat Pick, *Creaturely Poetics*, 11.
70 Wendell, *The Rejected Body*, 113.
71 Sharon Cameron, *Impersonality*, 124.

that is disposed *impersonally*.

Labor, useless suffering, disease, and energies made aimless by powers beyond my control all have the effect of wearing down my particular reference point, causing me to feel a bit like inert matter, anonymous and insignificant. Ironically, this is the condition for genuine solidarity and fellowship. Weil recalls an expression that workers and peasants have when an apprentice gets injured. They say, "It is the trade entering his body."[72] She understands this to be a metaphor for the connective potential of somatic pain: when I meet up against the brute reality of the world, whether through work or through refusal to inflict unjust harm onto others or through the impersonal forces of nature like disease, my *particular* body becomes a medium on which the *impersonal* truths of mortality, vulnerability, and by extension the needs of others are inscribed, facilitating an apprenticeship in loving attention. Indeed, Weil follows the previous quotation with:

> May all suffering make the universe enter into the body.
>
> Habit, skill: a transference of the consciousness into an object other than the body itself.
>
> May this object be the universe, the seasons, the sun, the stars.
>
> The relationship between the body and the tool changes during apprenticeship. We have to change the relationship between our body and the world. We do not become detached, we change our attachment. We must attach ourselves to the all.
>
> We have to feel the universe through each sensation.[73]

In other words, by attaching myself "to the all," I relinquish the perspective that is tied up with my preferences, tastes, and desires alone, and forge a bond with the many who do not share my opinions, privileges, cultural conditions, and perhaps even my species.[74]

72 Weil, *Waiting for God*, 78.

73 Weil, *Gravity and Grace*, 141.

74 In addition to Sunaura Taylor's recent book *Beasts of Burden: Animal and Disability Liberation*, Anat Pick's book, *Creaturely Poetics: Animality and Vulner-*

The attention that was initially bound up by my unflinching and consented encounter with pain has, as a result, established my bondage and kinship to the universe. If I am faithful to this connection, I suffer by the suffering of others with whom I do not necessarily share a personal relationship, and I cease to treat the most proximate beings as the most real. Weil offers an excellent illustration of this transition to an impersonal perspective in a religious context:

> A man whose whole family had died under torture, and who had himself been tortured for a long time in a concentration camp; or a sixteenth-century Indian, the sole survivor after the total extermination of his people. Such men if they had previously believed in the mercy of God would either believe in it no longer, or else they would conceive of it quite differently from before. I have not been through such things. I know, however, that they exist; so what is the difference?[75]

It seems technically possible for a person to arrive at such an impersonal perspective on a purely theoretical basis; after all, "the impersonal" has been traditionally equivocated with a priori reason, and abstraction has been sufficient to arrive at "impersonal" conclusions. However, Weil observed that such transmutations in attention were highly unlikely when the fantasies of limitlessness went unchallenged—i.e., in times of relative health, prosperity, unchecked power, and good fortune. The personal perspective and the purely "pragmatic" mode of attention obtain until the persistence of some difficulty violently interrupts our presumed self-sufficiency.

If such interruptions are not quickly rationalized or otherwise dismissed, and if I consent to the objectless void caused by (legiti-

ability in Literature and Film (New York: Columbia University Press, 2011) deals eloquently with the possibilities for human-animal connection in light of Weilian conceptions of vulnerability, or what Pick calls "creaturely exposure" (15). For extended treatments of Weil and animality, see: Beatrice Marovich, "Recreating the Creature: Weil, Agamben, Animality, and the Unsaveable," *Simone Weil and Continental Philosophy*, ed. Rebecca Rozelle-Stone (NY: Rowman and Littlefield, 2017).

75 Simone Weil, *Gravity and Grace*, 115.

mate) pains, my apprenticeship in attention progresses. I learn to see, touch, taste, and listen in newer and *more expansive* ways, for my sensibility has extended beyond the borders of my body to the world that I encounter. In the process of this development, I learn to endure the discordance between my desires and phenomena as given. My aversion to pain produces all manner of artifice, denial, and aggression as a mode of transference. But the aversion can and must be endured in such a way that I deprive myself of the imaginary objects. "It is better," as Weil says, "to say 'I am suffering' than 'this landscape is ugly.'"[76] How many acts of violence could be prevented by this simple recognition?

III. Conclusion

Simone Weil is unambiguous in her assessment of human pain and suffering: For her, it is an alien presence, indigestible, *absurd*: "To turn suffering into an offering [as with martyrdom] is a consolation, and it is thus a veil thrown over the reality of suffering. But the same applies if we regard suffering as punishment. Suffering has no significance. There lies the very essence of its reality."[77] Wendell would agree with this assessment, writing:

> I do not believe that I became ill *because* I needed to learn what illness has taught me, nor that I will get well when I have learned everything I need to know from it. We learn from many things that do not happen to us because we need to learn from them (to regard the death of a loved one, for example, as primarily a lesson for oneself, is hideously narcissistic), and many people who could benefit from learning the same things never have the experiences that would teach them.[78]

To truly experience that suffering merely *is*, that it has no *telos*, that it expresses nothing, and that we cannot ultimately avoid it, is to humbly consent to a mimetic silence ourselves. But this silence,

76 Ibid., 144.

77 Weil, *The Notebooks of Simone Weil*, trans. Arthur Wills (New York: Routledge, 2004), 483-484.

78 Wendell, *The Rejected Body*, 175.

so often a characteristic of the experience of pain, is not always negative or confining; silence can also be one of the most "valuable ways of being" effected by suffering, and be both generative and receptive.

Recall Stephen Grosz's patient, Anthony, who, over the course of his sessions following an HIV diagnosis, became more and more reticent on the couch. Grosz's responses to these silences and his education by his patient are telling. He writes:

> It is difficult for me to convey the feeling of these sessions—the overwhelming stillness and heaviness in the consulting room. There was nothing numbing about the silences; if anything, I listened more attentively. I sat forward, on the edge of my chair. There are silences that are anxious, where the patient—arms folded, eyes open—refuses to speak. There are uncomfortable silences, following a disclosure of something intimate or sexual, say. Anthony's silences were wholly different; he wasn't resisting or self-conscious. Under ordinary circumstances, I might ask a patient who has been silent for some time what they're thinking or feeling, and once or twice I did this with Anthony. But I soon realized that my speaking was an intrusion, a disturbance.[79]

As the meetings with Anthony continued, Grosz noted that the usual stabilizing signals he had come to rely upon in his sessions—both from his patients and from his own internal gauges—were disappearing. He explains, "After sitting with patients for thousands and thousands of hours, I'd developed an internal clock for fifty minutes. But with Anthony my clock broke."[80] These silences came to acquire a multitude of meanings for both analyst and analysand, but for Grosz, the most important aspect of the experi-

79 Stephen Grosz, *The Examined Life*, 200.

80 Ibid., 202. Weil recognizes that "the fragmentation of time" is "a characteristic of affliction." She writes along these lines: "Two thoughts lighten affliction a little. Either that it will stop almost immediately or that it will never stop. We can think of it as impossible or necessary, but we can never think that it simply is. That is unendurable. 'It is not possible!' What is not possible is to envisage a future where the affliction will continue. The natural spring of thought towards the future is arrested. We are lacerated in our sense of time" (Weil, *Gravity and Grace*, 82).

ence was that the silences "were something [they] went through together."[81]

This silence also confirms what we have long suspected: that the answers often provided to and for the afflicted are false, and we realize that, as Weil wrote, "there is a natural alliance between truth and affliction, because both of them are mute suppliants, eternally condemned to stand speechless in our presence."[82] By virtue of this accidental but material education, we might come to cultivate an attentive silence that "says more" than any of our attempted and obscene consolations could offer. This holds true whether the consolations are for another or for myself. (Indeed, too often the consolations inattentively offered to others have the primary function of consoling ourselves.) On Wendell's rereading of *Job*, a book which was also central to Weil's meditations on evil and suffering, Wendell notes that she was amused to discover that Job's friends and colleagues offered many (unsolicited) theories of how he had brought the plagues of misfortune upon himself, through his own actions and omissions. The story is a timeless and universal one that comes from the site of affliction but presents a moral, epistemic, and spiritual challenge for us all. Wendell articulates the challenge in words that Weil herself might have employed: "Can you love and seek to know Reality even if Reality might be like this?"[83]

81 Ibid., 205.

82 Weil, "Human Personality," *Simone Weil: An Anthology*, ed. Sian Miles (New York: Grove Press, 1986), 68.

83 Wendell, *The Rejected Body*, 108-109. [The original quote reads: "Can you love and seek to know God even if God might be like this? Eds.]

OBJECTS THAT MATTER

Bodies, Art, and Big Data

KATHERINE BEHAR INTERVIEWED BY ANNA MIRZAYAN

Katherine Behar's videos, performances, interactive installations, and writings explore gender and labor in digital culture. Associate Professor of New Media Arts at Baruch College, CUNY, Behar is the editor of Object-Oriented Feminism *(University of Minnesota Press, 2016), author of* Bigger than You: Big Data and Obesity *(punctum books, 2016), and coeditor (with Emmy Mikelson) of* And Another Thing: Nonanthropocentrism and Art *(punctum books, 2016). We would like to thank Prof. Behar for her generosity and intellect.*

‡ ‡ ‡

Anna Mirzayan: This issue of *Chiasma* is interested in embodiment, so I am wondering what kinds of bodies matter to you, what you see as the matter of bodies, and whether there is something the matter with notions of embodiment?

Katherine Behar: Excellent questions! What kinds of bodies matter? To start, I'm interested in how object-oriented theory and feminist thinking both share in common the idea that *all* bodies matter. Different feminisms have differently stressed the significance of embodiment, but primarily for human subjects. This has led to an understandably vexed relationship with the objectification of human bodies—and yes, I think there is something "the matter" with that anthropocentric or subject-oriented notion of embodiment. Object-oriented feminism does not mean to shirk the real situation of objectification. Instead, it lets us *also* consider all objects as having bodies already in their thingness, apart from objectification. This opens the question of bodies to matter that moves through all different scales. In this sense, the bodies that matter are just that—matter—although I prefer a slightly less rarified term like "stuff." Brought together in OOF, new materialist and object-oriented thinking ask that bodies be reconceived to maintain embodiment as a locus of feminist politics, but precisely by engaging the politics around objectification that marks bodies as such. In the same way that we might wish to expand our feminist solidarities, I am interested in expansively reconceiving the body to apply broadly to matter at all scales.

AM: What do you see as the matter of bodies—what makes up bodies? A very difficult question…

KB: That *is* a really hard question. I don't know that I will have a satisfactory answer, in part because I feel as though we're historically at a moment when a shift is underway, and this shifting makes that question an especially slippery one just now.

For example, one way to conceive of bodies is as having a wholeness to them, right? In this way of thinking about a body, it's something that has form, and there comes a point where the form of one thing ends and the next thing begins. You could put it this way: a body is a body that has a continuity with itself. But already that's not as simple as it sounds. For one thing, this continuity also encompasses diversity. For instance, the human body contains zillions of diverse parts (a philosopher might say "we contain multitudes")—from organs to organisms and from elements to waste—and of course these parts also have bodies of their own. So a single body can contain diverse matter. But, just the same, if we can recognize any body as a body, it's because of its continuity of form.

One thing I've been thinking about lately is that this kind

of continuity—formal continuity—has a reference to the analog. A form, or a shape, or an expanse—whatever you want to call it—has its own wholeness, which we acknowledge in our willingness to recognize its contours, or its material consistency, or even its identity (a big word). That kind of continuity has an analog dimension. If the digital is a technology for dividing, then the wholeness of bodies—exactly their indivisibility—is both what "makes them up," in answer to your question, and what makes them analog.

But I just mentioned a shift underway, and it's this: one of the things that I think is happening currently, and that I am trying to engage with in the work I'm doing now, is that the digital may be infiltrating bodies. I mean, in a material sense, we've been cyborgs for a long time. Now, I am interested in an abstracted sense of infiltration, an infiltration in intuition. The digital is a way of dividing, of making things separate, discrete, and discontinuous, like the hard cut between one and zero. I think the analog continuity of bodies is becoming divided differently now. Bodies are becoming internally divided. And as a result, bodies are also gaining the potential for becoming externally or transbodily recomposed.

AM: What you were saying about infiltration and multiplicity, as opposed to thinking about the person or the figure as this one bounded thing, reminds me of the talk you gave, "Personalities Without People." In that talk, you suggested something worrisome: that data profiles used by big companies for targeted advertising and political targeting of voters via their online presence were using the same principles being valorized by a lot of intersectional feminism. Could you talk about that connection as well as some alternative feminisms that might avoid this connection?

KB: Yes, in my research into the practices of data platforms like Facebook and Google, and data firms like Cambridge Analytica, I've observed what I see as a disturbing technical parallel with intersectionality. There's a way in which data collection and data mining, which are core operations for the corporate mercenary capitalist tech sector, carry the same logics as intersectional feminism. In both, the main idea is a complete accounting of individuals through as many different data points as possible, with the assumption that more data points, especially from unusual or improbable intersections, will better specify the complexity of an individual and better predict identity. So I posed a question in that talk, and I posed it partly in a tongue-in-cheek manner but also quite seriously—I asked whether intersectionality is "woke data-mining."

I asked this because I think a founding principle—that we are constituted through many intersections of data points—is the same. Plus, they both presume the total disclosure of those data points. And through that disclosure, both arrive at a technical conception of identity as identifiability. More and more intersections of data points will produce a unique profile of an individual because the specific pattern of intersections is what uniquely defines identity. There are many things we could say about the underlying assumptions in conceiving identity through identifiability—not the least of which is that it takes as given that all individuals must render themselves fully transparent to data harvesting procedures that grow ever more obsessively minute.

Yet my main point in making this observation is not to say that this makes intersectional feminism bad or conversely that data mining could be a good thing because its principles are shared by intersectional feminists whose politics we may admire. I'm not interested in evaluating these things one way or the other. What I am interested in is how the same procedures appear across the board and on both ends of the political spectrum, so my sense is that it's both and neither. In fact, I would say it's a symptom of the same shift I was talking about earlier, from a continuous, analog body to a divided, fractured one.

In "Personalities Without People,"[1] I related this divisibility to the independence of secondary qualities in object-oriented theory. This is the idea that attributes of objects, which previously

1 Behar, Katherine. "Personalities Without People," Panel Presentation, *Tuning Speculation V: Vibratory (Ex)changes*. The Occulture, Toronto, Ontario, Canada, November 18, 2017.

marked objects' identities, are now objects in their own right. To take the example of human objects, secondary qualities like gender, race, class, nationality, and so on, are now radically detached from that class of objects we call subjects, which these attributes allegedly once defined. This is one way that analog bodies are becoming internally divided. And as their defining characteristics are stripped away, those attributes are reconstituted into transhuman metrics with their own political agency.

As you might guess, what I *would* critique or say is "bad" (in too coarse a term) is how in both contexts—intersectional feminism and corporate data mining—the reliance on the heightened detail and specificity of intersectional data profiles is being applied in ways that tend toward breaking down communication and commonality. Some recent intersectional debates have demanded matching data points as a precondition for the right to speak, resulting in a total breakdown of communication. It's just like social media filter bubbles. I call this "intersectionality done badly," though I want to be clear that I am a proponent of intersectional feminisms. While historically feminist, anti-racist, and anti-capitalist movements have all at times benefited from strategic autonomy, what troubles me in certain instances today is something that looks less like autonomy and more like dismissal.

There are many examples of this in art and academia, most often taking the form of calls for censorship that bluntly refuse to hear alternative perspectives on the basis that a person coming from a different background can't speak to someone's condition because they don't have a perfectly symmetrical set of data points. If we dismiss someone's right to speak about anything other than their own experience, and to anyone other than those who share the same attributes of experience, we will end up with people only talking to themselves or those sufficiently "like" themselves. And let's not forget that the end point of these data practices is uniquely identified individuals, so in a very real sense, this logical trajectory culminates in people talking only to themselves. Intersectionality done badly is this breakdown of communication. To my thinking intersectionality should motivate us to do the hard work of finding common ground while acknowledging difference; difference should not, in my opinion, be taken as a justification to refuse communication entirely.

In the case of data mining practices, there is another concern. Data mining requires massive data collection—which for me amounts to a kind of pathological hoarding—and in its very presence this overgrowth contributes to the rise of big data as a cultural norm. Nobody was talking about big data ten years ago, but now it's common practice. But another common practice that is not often remarked upon is the fact that the retention or accumulation of data also requires data reduction. So what I see happening in practices like personality profiling, is hyper-specificity turning into caricature. All of this alleged specificity ends up pushing people's political views to extremes that are in all senses of the word "reductive." An algorithm takes somebody who might be moderate, or at least nuanced, and gives them the data feed of somebody who is far more politically extreme. This is marketed as "personalization," but it actually means lumping people together on the basis of a particular data-mined factor that might connect them.

AM: *Feeding* them data?

KB: If you think of something like News*feed*, it is, right?

AM: I was literally just reading your piece on obesity and big data!

KB: Right. That's exactly the overgrowth that I am talking about.

AM: I was really interested in what you were just saying about hyper-specificity and profiling. In this piece you talk about that, alongside becoming so large that one becomes vague or imperceptible, and about Lauren Berlant's slow death and lateral agency in *Cruel Optimism*. I am wondering if you could speak more to that as a strategy. I immediately was thinking about Alex Galloway's informatic opacity, or the way it's taken up by Zach Blas who queers this idea of opacity, and finds a really interesting art practice with it.

But I also see pitfalls to this strategy. So I am just wondering what you think about imperceptibility and vagueness.

KB: Well, I'm in favor! [laughs] There are pitfalls to all of our strategies, and while I don't want to romanticize failure, I am okay with going down a wrong path, or adopting a faulty strategy, in the sense that object-oriented feminism is ready to be wrong. But in all seriousness, I do think that we need strategies to become more imperceptible now, and these strategies will also rail against the notions of identity *and* identifiability. Blas's work is interesting in this respect. Whether we adopt opacity following Glissant or imperceptibility following Grosz, I think this is extremely important right now, when we risk becoming over-identified through the surveillance state.

AM: In this long essay, fatness becomes a technique of embodied vagueness, and you refer to it as abstraction that draws on the plasticity both of bodies and of data. This process is framed as "getting over oneself" and then becoming imperceptible. But it could also be said that abstraction is the change from use value to generic exchange value, and it is thus the founding move of capitalism. Do you see any sort of tension between that kind of embodied abstraction and capitalist abstraction?

KB: That is so interesting. I was invoking abstraction from the perspective of art and the abstracted image, but you're correct. As you say, it is "embodied abstraction" that provides the connection between abstraction in imagery and abstraction in capitalism. For example, "getting over oneself" allows the devaluation of self that comes with generic exchangeability. Rather than self-commodification or selling oneself in the neoliberal sense, it's about becoming off-brand, generic, and featureless. It's like cutting out your label. This devaluation sounds grim, and it is, but it seems to me that we are in a race to the bottom whether we volunteer to cut out our own "self" labels or not. So to speak of strategies again, it's worth considering whether there may be benefits to doing so, whether there's something to be gained from self-effacement. And I always go back to that saying that it's always easier to envision the end of the world than the end of capitalism.

But this is also where object-oriented feminism has a stake. In a very real, not abstract, not metaphoric sense, humans are objects and are objects of exchange in this capitalist moment. And although I am talking about a contemporary phenomenon when I am discussing abstraction in data, we should remember that capitalism (not to mention the entire modernist enterprise!) was founded on racist objectification in slavery. We don't get to contemporary capitalism without humans' being objects and commodities first. Human objecthood is part and parcel of capitalism's founding gestures, if you will. Nevertheless, part of why I think the object-oriented theories of the last ten years struck a chord was because in this late capitalist moment, we see plainly that we are living in networks that make our exchangeability a lived experience. It's not a haunting notion, or a fear, or a paranoia that we *might* be exchangeable. We *are* exchangeable, and we are living that experience and are reminded of it constantly by the infrastructures of everyday life. Maybe that's what lent it a sense of the ontological—that feeling that this is the nature of being. But I think that's wrong. Object-orientation is *not* ontological because it's historical—it's specific to the world that we're living in now, which is a capitalist world permeated by data and networks.

Part of what I am interested in, coming from *Bigger than You*,[2] is that our marketplace exchangeability with other humans also logically permits exchangeability between humans and nonhuman machines. We see this in the automation of labor; we see this in the automation of cognitive processes; we see this in our social networks. Most often this exchangeability is framed negatively, positioning nonhumans as a competitive threat to humans. But I am interested in reframing exchangeability as evidence of human/nonhuman closeness—and I am interested in what may come out of that closeness. Going back to your earlier question, "what is the

2 Behar, Katherine. *Bigger than You: Big Data and Obesity: An Inquiry towards Decelerationist Aesthetics*. Earth, Milky Way: punctum books, 2016.

matter of bodies?", this is an opportunity to rethink. Maybe the matter of bodies has the consistency of data? Maybe there's something porous about that? That porosity, that diffuseness, could open up a kind of resistance, in terms of passively cloaking or infusing ourselves with the diffuseness of otherness, and in terms of active solidarities between humans and nonhumans. To have solidarity with nonhumans—in fact, to have solidarity at all right now—is an act of resistance. It's also a way to obfuscate identity and loosen neoliberal capitalism's requisite fetishization of individualism (that is only further operationalized when identity becomes identifiability). Redrawing the contours of our profiles is an important practice of resistance now. It is an opportunity to be more generous in what we include as mattering *to* us and in what we incorporate in the mattering *of* us.

AM: I really like the way you seem to be expanding or bloating the idea of species.

KB: I love that. "Bloating" the notion of species—yes!

AM: Well in the OOF book (I like saying OOF) you talk about the danger of requiring all these connections—connected vitalism. It's really interesting to think about what sort of connections or solidarities you *are* advocating for that are not these networked, web-like notions. Instead there are all those little drawings in *Bigger than You* around data points. It's as though the blob is somehow a better visualization than the net. But it also seems like it's really difficult to navigate the kinds of connections you want to advocate for and the kinds you see as problematic. How did you make that distinction?

KB: I'm an artist, so it's my prerogative—and in fact my job—to make and remake and unmake. So for me those distinctions must constantly be redrawn. It's about changing one's mind or making up one's mind afresh, as much as it's about art practice. I am sure you're familiar with the famous illustrations in Paul Baran's proposal for distributed packet switching networks. The drawings depict centralized, decentralized, and distributed networks as dots with lines connecting them. This is the way network topologies are usually visualized: with nodes and edges as dots and lines. One of the things that in principle underlies the operationality of those kinds of networks is that you can swap the dots and the lines around, and the idea of the distributed network is that you can get rid of one dot and replace it with another dot. This is what Baran calls "redundancy." It's what makes a network robust, and it's exactly the exchangeability that I'm talking about. But to enable exchangeability between dots or nodes requires lines or edges. And what I am trying to get at in those drawings in *Bigger than You* is to visualize what would happen if we get rid of the lines and think of those dots as having materiality and substance? What is a network that is all nodes and no edges? It would be an information network at near standstill, and would be an instance of what I call "decelerationist aesthetics." In the drawings, I am sketching this question: What aesthetic form would that take and how would that form *perform*? While I was writing *Bigger than You,* I was also working on a video series, *Modeling Big Data.* In those videos I perform as the obese body of big data. The form or the whole extent of my body physically circumscribes my performative capacities and those capacities will differ as concerns my obese data body, versus my flexible worker body, versus my body at rest, and so on.

In terms of navigating what kinds of connections are beneficial or harmful, I think it is also important ongoing work to keep making and remaking our value statements. For example, the rhizomatic distributed network looked radically emancipatory in recent memory, but now when I look at those network drawings from Baran, I no longer think so. They show that from the perspective of the network, a dot doesn't exist unless it's plugged in. A node isn't a node unless it has at least one edge. That kind of compulsory connectivity is something I want to question. I am not interested in advocating for or against one form or another, but rather in conceptualizing what kinds of affordances and constraints these different material forms may present. So what happens if we erase those compulsory edges?

AM: You say, I think very correctly, that the dot doesn't exist unless it's plugged in, in this schema. You have the idea of geometry in that part of that *Bigger than You* essay. The very first axiom of Euclid's *Elements* is "a point is that which has no part." So it doesn't *exist*, but it also *has* to exist because points connect lines, right? I was trying to read shifts in the sorts of geometries and maths and spaces that you're making available via rethinking connectivity as the opening up of new political spaces. Maybe non-Euclidean space is a new political space that we just haven't mined yet because we don't think of our bodies as anything but three or four dimensional.

KB: I think you're absolutely right.

AM: I am really happy that you brought up decelerationist aesthetics because I am so interested in the connection between OOF and the sort of joking sound of "OOF" and exhaustion and spreading out—how do you mobilize exhaustion? How do you see that happening?

KB: How do we mobilize exhaustion... that's all we've got, right? That could be our most pressing question, because we're at a point of fatigue and collapse and even exhausted outrage where it's always "the final straw." This is another place where I depart from accelerationist thinkers. There's simply too much collapse all around us right now, so I am definitely not seeking to push capitalism further to collapse more. There is a toll for this collapse and I think it's really irresponsible to disregard that harm. What I would prefer is to find a way to mobilize from within this sensibility and experience of collapse and exhaustion in order to try to extend care. If there is a new non-Euclidean political space coming out of this, I hope it's a space of care.

AM: Is part of the appeal of turning to human and non-human

connectivities learning new modes of care?

KB: Yes.

AM: I wonder about trying to figure out decelerationist aesthetics in the political landscape where something like nostalgia and slowing-down has been so mobilized by the right or by neo-conservatism. It seems tricky to talk about speeds. I am wondering whether it was tricky for you.

KB: Um… Nope! [laughs] I mean, that's become an accelerationist term, like localism, in the argument that nostalgic, slow localism has been coopted. But for me honestly no, I don't have a hard time making a distinction with speed. And I believe firmly in the localism of Donna Haraway's situated knowledges. I am willing to go out on a limb and say this quite flatly: I think that we need to slow down. I see too many examples of negative effects and negative affects associated with acceleration. And it's unquestionably the dominant pace, so it deserves rethinking, if only to challenge its hegemony.

AM: I am pretty much on board with that. I've read some people speaking about some of your artworks, *E-Waste*[3] specifically, and it being referred to as a bit archeological, and also a bit paternalistic because of the way care was being read like a parent cares for the child. And to me your work was really playful and goofy—I mean in a project like *Roomba Rumba*, Roombas are so goofy and I don't think you can ever escape that; and even perverse, like sticking together the organic and the inorganic. And I was thinking about that while reading your Botox article in the *Object-Oriented Feminism*[4] collection. Of course then you started talking about necrophilia vs. vivophilia, and you can't not intend the inevitably grotesque as-

3 Behar, Katherine. *E-Waste*, 2014. Solo exhibition with catalogue. Tuska Center for Contemporary Art at the University of Kentucky.

4 Behar, Katherine. "Facing Necrophilia, or 'Botox Ethics'," in *Objected-Oriented Feminism*, edited by Katherine Behar. Minneapolis: University of Minnesota Press, 2016.

sociations with that, right? And then you discuss ORLAN's plastic surgery art practice, blurring the lines between death and playfulness and beauty… It all seems so perverse.

KB: Why, thank you!

AM: Yeah! I am wondering if perversion plays into decelerationist aesthetics at all.

KB: It's a really great association.

AM: Obese bodies are so often thought of as perverse, right?

KB: That's exactly right. Yes! I had not made that connection. I think a lot about perversion. (Does that makes me sound like a pervert?) I think perversion and perversity are important resources to draw from. Perversity was mobilized by avant-gardist traditions (mostly Western white male) insofar as art's irrationality offers some kind of perverse alternative to rationalist society. But I am most interested in the very important work of feminist body artists who took on perversion in a directly embodied way. This brings us back to your original question about embodiment, because in feminist body art, perversion is an embodied practice of making, remaking, and unmaking. The female body was (and is) already a socially perverse object, so in feminist body art, artists took up perversion by way of their own actual bodies as always already perverse. For me, this work is so important because that perversion becomes inseparable from the perversity of feminist authorship to begin with.

In making, remaking, and unmaking, it also gets into Catherine Malabou's notion of plasticity, which I talk about in "Facing Necrophilia, or 'Botox Ethics'" regarding ORLAN's work. I wrote this essay before coming up with the term, so I did not explicitly connect "Facing Necrophilia" with decelerationist aesthetics, but I absolutely agree with you. Decelerationist aesthetics is very much there in the double role Botox plays as an inhibitor of communication and as an aesthetic or cosmetic body practice. There's something disruptive about perversion, and one might leverage that disruptive power of the perverse to gum up the machine and the acceleration of capital. That said, I also want to move against the avant-garde model that uses the perverse as shock value to shock the bourgeois sensibility. Because we've had enough [laughs]. Just like we have enough collapse, we have enough shock. Shock value is just Twitter. It is completely in tune with acceleration. But there's something about a slower experience of embodied perversion, which is much more in line with what I want to draw out—as a decelerationist time frame—and draw forth—as decelerationist politics. There are aesthetic forms we can adopt that I think can give us that direction.

‡ REVIEWS

WORD TOYS: POETRY AND TECHNICS

By Brian Kim Stefans, Tuscaloosa: University of Alabama Press, 2017

JOHN NYMAN

Printed on a ream of unbound (and mostly blank) paper, Kenneth Goldsmith's 2015 *Theory*—a collage of anecdotes, quotations, and provocations largely recycled from his now decades-long career as an "uncreative" writer[1]—may best personify the coupling of formally experimental poetry and high theory after the turn of the current century. In short, *Theory* is vapid, self-indulgent, suspiciously marketable, and deeply unsatisfying. And while more nuanced argumentation has emerged, even flourished, in less spot lit corners of contemporary poetic criticism, much of it either falls back on the shopworn methods of conventional (i.e., late twentieth-century) literary scholarship or leans hard on supplanting aesthetic provocateurism with hands-on activism.

In the midst of these polemics, Brian Kim Stefans's *Word Toys* is a shining star—or, to honour his prevailing theme of *text as technicity*, an asterisk. While maintaining the passion for the artistically alien that remains, in my view, avant-garde criticism's foremost reason for being, Stefans is explicitly sensitive to experimental literature's historical, cultural, and intellectual situations. The result is a study that is neither devotional nor reactionary, but genuinely interesting. Stefans seeks primarily to connect the post-hermeneutic philosophies of thinkers such as Alain Badiou, Gilbert Simondon, and Bernard Stiegler to the literary lineage ex-

1 Kenneth Goldsmith, *Theory* (Paris, Jean Boîte Éditions, 2013).

tending through Poundian modernism and Charles Olson's "open field" to the poetries of both the early internet and Web 2.0; in the process, however, *Word Toys* illuminates a kaleidoscopic catalogue of technologies—including prehistoric clay currency, nineteenth-century nomograms (two-dimensional drawings used to assist with complex computational operations), and esoteric programming languages—as well as literary artworks—such as Christian Bök's 'pataphysical poetry, Xu Bing's "Square Word Calligraphy" (a system for rendering English words in the visual style of Chinese ideography), and the early internet writer Toadex Hobogrammathon's "Dagmar Chili" anti-blog. This index might suggest that *Word Toys* is among the chaotic textual assemblages Stefans dubs "undigests"—almanacs or sourcebooks more suited to perusal than focused study or debate—and there is some truth in that depiction, with Stefans himself describing several of his chapters as "overloaded with concepts."[2] But Stefans's humility is outpaced by his simultaneously thorough and visionary understanding of theory; if previous generations of avant-garde poets were always only inspired by philosophical ideas, Stefans is among the first to master them. While the arguments elaborated in *Word Toys* are not airtight, they are immensely compelling, helping to lay the groundwork for a newly historicized understanding of poetic composition in the age of the internet.

Stefans is unequivocal in placing continental philosophy at the forefront of his approach to poetry, as his explanations of philosophical concepts consistently overshadow both historical contextualization and textual analysis or "close reading." Yet Stefans also evades the conventional method of theory-driven criticism, which sets philosophy in the role of a frame, lens, or system henceforth used to digest the texts under consideration. In contrast, Stefans's discussions of philosophical concepts, representative literary works, and historical case studies (each of which is more or less complete in itself) are planted side by side, jostling against each other like billiard balls or tectonic plates. The style can be grating

2 Brian Kim Stefans, *Word Toys: Poetry and Technics* (Tuscaloosa: University of Alabama Press, 2017), 9.

at times (especially in the book's later chapters, where transitions, summaries, and syntheses become increasingly sparse), but generally fits well with Stefans's argument, which maintains that poems are *evental* in the sense described by Badiou. Rather than existing through their relationships with subjects or meanings already rendered possible within the world, they are singular objects with their own truths, essences, and forms of becoming. At some points, this means that poems are uniquely linked to Gilles Deleuze and Félix Guattari's "plane of immanence," in which the undifferentiated energy of being gives rise to an endless virtuality of novel forms. However, Stefans more frequently posits poetry in the mode of Simondon's *technicity*, a category populated by inorganic yet evolving individuals deeply engaged in the pursuit of life "by means other than life."[3] The book's titular "toys" are less often playthings than sites of technical activity in the vein of William Carlos Williams's "machine[s] made of words."[4] Or, following a somewhat different tack that links poetry to the mathematical truth value of graphs and diagrams, they are "transitional objects" in the sense proposed by D. W. Winnicott (via Stiegler): that is, foundational tools for navigating the threshold between the interior of the subject and the unknowable externality Quentin Meillassoux calls "the great outdoors."

Among the many concepts Stefans addresses throughout *Word Toys* (and there really are a lot of them), his application of technicity to poetic composition is especially fruitful for two reasons. First, the recognition that technical objects, like living organisms, have a *function* establishes a continuum between radically open or "indeterminate" experimental poetries and those that are more linear, closed, or "undecidable" (in that they involve "not the *blurring* of meanings but the flipping back and forth or between several discrete meanings [...] one of which must be chosen to make a poem work").[5] Second, Stefans's insistence on approaching poems non-hermeneutically, as the sites of concrete "reality effects" akin

3 Stefans, *Word Toys*, 69.
4 Ibid., 67.
5 Ibid., 27.

to practical applications of technology,[6] connects poem-objects to the machines and algorithms whose operations more obviously determine the shape of the modern world. In both of these respects, Stefans offers a compelling alternative to the views of Language poets and poet-scholars such as Charles Bernstein, whose ideas he also deftly critiques. For Bernstein and his colleagues, formal experimentation is justified by a Manichean opposition between linguistic indeterminacy and semantic closure, where the latter characterizes both conventional poetics and the capitalist paradigm of the commodity. Yet the observation (not unique to Stefans) that Language poetry "seems to imitate, rather than combat or resist, the logics of late capitalism"[7] indicates the ultimate impotence of the Language poets' radical-normative binary. In contrast, Stefans's technicity suggests that avant-garde forms evolve from conventional forms according to their own essences and intentionalities, potentially unmooring them from binary opposition and capitalistic exchange. Although Stefans's theory could be described as conservative—because it consciously rewinds philosophy to a time before the "linguistic turn," and because it posits a gradient or grey area between avant-garde and hegemonic aesthetics—it is a vital response to Goldsmith's and other post-Language avant-garde writers' spectacular failure to balance experimental poetics and radical politics.

In the realm of literary criticism more broadly, Stefans's commitment to a form of reading that eschews hermeneutics (i.e., the analysis of transmitted meanings) is probably his most remarkable accomplishment. Taking his inspiration from Graham Harman's and Meillassoux's adherence to a "naive mimesis" in their readings of H. P. Lovecraft and Stéphane Mallarmé,[8] Stefans is able to consistently bracket the question of interpretability as he instead emphasizes the concrete acts—including speculation, computation, and un-grounding—that both poems and readers perform in their navigations of language and the universe. For ex-

6 Ibid., 23.
7 Ibid., 116.
8 Ibid., 3.

ample, his discussion of information theorist Claude Shannon's "27th letter"—in layman's terms, a blank space, such as the space between two words—elucidates the poetic value of non-meaning without making ambiguity an end in itself: rather than signifying pure ineffability, the blank space "*works*" by engaging the (human or mechanical) reader in "a statistical analysis of the future events of the poem," an action whose dynamism constitutes the positive content of the poem itself.[9] On the other hand, the strength of Stefans's proposals is sometimes undermined by the extreme breadth of his subject matter, especially when he attempts the older-school literary critical endeavours of classification and canon-formation. In both his three-part breakdown of "speculative prosody" and his taxonomy of "outsider writing," Stefans fails to convincingly reconcile traditional schemes (such as Roman Jakobson's self-referentiality or John Ashberry's "other tradition") with the digital literatures his study celebrates. Between the various essays collected in *Word Toys*, it remains unclear whether Stefans intends to characterize all poetry as a species of technicity or simply to highlight those poetries that are among the most technically inclined.

This muddying, in turn, sets up one of the most intractable problems facing *Word Toys* and its line of argument. Stefans's fifth chapter—titled "Terrible Engines" and acting as a sort of critical centre of the book—begins by adding a third to Brian McHale's description of the modernist and postmodernist literary "dominants." While modernism's "epistemological dominant" interrogated the human subject's relationship with reality, and postmodernism's "ontological dominant" challenged the reality of the subject itself, Stefans proposes a speculative literature that bypasses their shared morass by "subjecting readers directly to the work and putting objects for study in their hands, both literally and figuratively."[10] The problem lies in the fact that these three paradigms cannot subsist in a genuine continuity, despite Stefans's earnest desire to see them do so. Instead, Stefans's "literature of sets," actualized mostly in the form of conceptualist games whose

9 Ibid., 42.
10 Ibid., 158-59.

rules are the concretes facts of language, recast modernist and post-modernist questioning as an objectless diversion. After all, the psychological and ludological theories on which Stefans relies (at least in parts of *Word Toys*) take for granted the actual existence of subject-players. If not a hard break, then, the relationship between McHale's and Stefans's literatures is marked by the overarching dominance of the latter, since modernism and post-modernism would have merely "acclimatized a human readership to ontological uncertainty" without having truly doubted the presence of that readership or the status of its humanity.[11] This impasse between speculative realism and what has been aptly called the "hermeneutics of suspicion" may very well be endemic to Stefans's sources in Badiou and Meillassoux. However, Stefans's attempt to overcome it in the field of literature—which, being fundamentally rooted in human language and culture, is inevitably populated by writers and readers for whom the function of *meaning* is hardly trivial—draws out some of its most compelling contradictions.

Overall, though, my challenge does not constitute a criticism of *Word Toys* so much as a way of positioning it within the diverse sets of texts, techniques, and technologies it assembles. To invoke an old distinction, Stefans is a writer who thinks through theories rather than facts, but his adventurousness usually serves him well. *Word Toys* engages many more concepts than I can adequately address, including many of Stefans's own creation and several that are provocative beyond the disciplinary confines of avant-garde literary criticism. In "Miscegenated Scripts," for example, Stefans braids Western (mis)conceptions of Asian cultural forms with pan-Asian experimental text art to posit a "transpacific" "algorithmic culture" that both draws from and cuts through ethnic identity.[12] This subject alone, with its encyclopaedic scope and bold implications, seems generative enough to spawn another 350 pages. But even if *Word Toys* evades any obvious unity of form, its sections gel into a unity of effect that is both subtle and impactful. In a milieu where both of Stefans's key fields—avant-garde po-

11 Ibid., 189.
12 Ibid., 193.

etry and continental philosophy—have seen their relevance diminish in accordance with their becoming increasingly tone-deaf and arcane, Stefans resuscitates their nuance and magic in the service of a practical wisdom with broad value to scholars both within and on the margins of his disciplines' traditional stomping grounds.

IN-BETWEEN: LATINA FEMINIST PHENOMENOLOGY, MULTIPLICITY, AND THE SELF

By Mariana Ortega, Albany, NY: SUNY Press, 2016

HELEN FIELDING

Mariana Ortega provides a detailed and much-needed account of multiplicitous selfhood drawing on Latina philosophy from an existential and phenomenological perspective. Certainly this monograph is a major contribution to Latina philosophy and Latina feminist phenomenology, as well as to feminist phenomenology and phenomenology more generally. One of the strengths of phenomenology has been the way it moves between the particular and the general, but, as Ortega points out, even existential phenomenological accounts "that profess to do justice to lived experience avoid personal descriptions informed by particular social identities, staying within the confines of general categories of existence."[1] To stay within such general categories not only fails to provide for the kinds of thick phenomenological accounts that enrich our understanding of the particularities of lived experience, but also of the generalities that allow us to understand more clearly what it means to be existentially human. Indeed, attending to thick descriptions of lived existence has led Ortega to extend phenomenological categories and understanding at the level of generality, providing us with her important concepts of living in-between worlds, and in particular, of multiple selves. But what Ortega accomplishes here is even more profound. In developing her concept of the multi-

1 Mariana Ortega, *In-Between: Latina Feminist Phenomenology, Multiplicity, and the Self* (Albany, N.Y.: SUNY Press, 2016), 2.

plicitous self she shows how the study of Latina feminist phenomenology is not a marginal—a subset of feminist phenomenology, or phenomenology in general—but rather completely changes the field. She reveals how what appear to be general and neutral accounts are in fact impoverished ones that do not phenomenologically reveal contemporary experiences of marginalized and oppressed selves who live between worlds.

For feminist phenomenology, Ortega's multiplicitous self allows for the appearance of that which is covered over, providing a critical methodological understanding of what it means to develop accounts of marginalized and oppressed selves, which is surely at the heart of feminist theorizing. Not only does this self allow for the necessary critical distance from the transcendental self of classical phenomenology that seems to presume a neutral embodied subject, but, more than this, Ortega intrinsically changes the way we understand the phenomenal self.

Ortega is, in Gloria Anzaldúa's sense, a new *mestiza* thinker as she is "embodied and situated in a particular space where particular economic, cultural, and historical circumstances crisscross."[2] This means that although the new *mestiza* thinker might "tactically" take on identities or thinking strategies, they cannot be chosen at will—they come out of her roots and lived experience. For Ortega the thinker, those roots are Latina philosophy and Heideggerian existential phenomenology, which she courageously thinks together. This move is courageous since, given Martin Heidegger's politics, it does not seem his thinking has, at first glance, anything to offer those opposed to oppression. Moreover, Latina philosophy, which rejects the unified subject, is not formally recognized within the traditional philosophical (and Eurocentric) classroom. But as an uncompromising *mestiza* thinker Ortega cannot but write what seems ethically demanded of her.

In-Between shows us why exploring this intersection between Heidegger and Latina philosophy can be so fruitful, and could only be initiated by a philosopher like Ortega who is herself a multiplicitous self, and so is able to bring together disparate per-

2 Ibid., 45.

spectives and think them together. The world-travelling her multiplicitousness requires of her allows her to see how "both Latina feminist phenomenological accounts of the self and existential phenomenological accounts have various similarities, the most important being the commitment to provide an account of selfhood that does justice to lived experience."[3] The Latina thinkers whose works she addresses, such as Anzaldúa, Maria Lugones and Chela Sandoval, might not think of their work as phenomenological nor do they employ formal phenomenological methodologies as such. Nonetheless, their rich descriptions of subjectivity expressed through the lens of each's lived experience are inherently phenomenological, and the theorizing that comes out of these descriptions overlaps with the phenomenological tradition, even as there are also significant differences. As Ortega describes it, "their appeal to experience is a disclosure, a making visible, audible, a making perceptible, those beings in marginalized and nondominant positions whose histories have been previously erased, ignored or covered up."[4]

Disclosure is of course the heart of phenomenology, making visible what was obscured, and recognizing that there is always that which cannot be collapsed into one frame of understanding. These descriptions also reveal that our philosophies need to take seriously not only the critiques of the unitary notions of the self, but moreover, if we are to understand oppression, living on the margins as well as resistance, we need theories that help explain the multiplicitous self. Understanding this phenomenon also contributes to understanding how we become selves and are selves.

In particular, Ortega explores the overlap between Heidegger and Anzaldúa. Like Anzaldúa's, Heidegger's self is not a substantial self but is rather relational. Humans do not have an essence that determines who they are in advance. They become who they are through the relations in which they engage, through their commitments and through their embodied situations. Nonetheless, as Ortega points out, though Heidegger explains the "major onto-

3 Ibid., 6.
4 Ibid., 7.

logical existential characteristics of a self" that is thrown into the world, "he does not explain the specific ontic situations" that selves live, specificities provided by the Latina thinkers Ortega engages.[5] Further, for both Anzaldúa and Heidegger, it is through anxiety that the "self becomes capable of ultimately making choices that are not expected or prescribed."[6] For Heidegger, anxiety reveals how the self is uncanny, or *unheimlich*, not at home in the world; it is a mood "that discloses the possibilities of being-in-the-world and the individual aspects of the self." For Anzaldúa, however, anxiety can lead to paralysis, since the *mestiza* self must grapple with the inability to make "extremely difficult choices given her multiple positionalities."[7] But both the experiences of not feeling at home, and of paralysis can lead to important critical reflection. Indeed Ortega describes how, along the way, she herself experienced periods of paralysis in her writing about the self.

In short, out of her engagement with Latina thinkers for whom the lived experiences of marginalization, oppression and resistance are central, as well as with Heidegger for whom the self is in the world, Ortega develops her own understanding of the multiplicitous self. This self is not a plural self, a self that moves from one perspective to the next, which is Lugones' understanding of world-travelling as Ortega describes it, nor is it a deep self that crosses all these experiences. Instead, it is a self between worlds. Drawing more specifically on Heidegger's existential phenomenology, for whom the self is always already in the world, always already a self shaped through spatio-temporal relations and commitments in the world into which she is thrown, for Ortega, the multiplicitous self is a "being-between-worlds and a being-in-worlds, an in-between self."[8]

As a good phenomenologist Ortega provides a number of descriptions of this multiplicitous self. For example, drawing from the work of Anzaldúa, the multiplicitous self "is a self inhabit-

5 Ibid., 54-55.
6 Ibid., 54.
7 Ibid., 54.
8 Ibid., 50.

ing the borderlands, a self in-between the U.S. and Mexico, who experiences a lived struggle because she is split between cultures, races, languages, and genders, all tugging at her, pulling her to one side or the other, demanding alliances or setting down rules, continually pushing her to choose one or the other, to suffer from an absolute despot duality."[9] But the multiplicitous self does not choose one or the other, and instead breaks down any binary approach that requires such a choice. For the multiplicitous self is "intersectional, flexible and tactical."[10]

Ortega engages with a number of Latina philosophers as she further specifies her understanding of this multiplicitous self. Thus, for example, though Maria Lugones's work is important to her own, Ortega distinguishes her multiplicitous self from what she understands as Lugones's ontological pluralism whereby 'world travelling' is defined for Lugones as "the experience of being different in different worlds", "an epistemic shift to other worlds of sense." By contrast, Ortega's multiplicitous self is embodied by the experience of living between worlds, "a practice of both survival and resistance" for those in the margins. According to this ontological pluralism, selves "experience themselves as different persons in different worlds." They do not "experience an underlying 'I'" that exists across these different worlds.[11] For Ortega, ontological pluralism would imply a multiplicity of selves and worlds "anchored in multiple realities," which ultimately is self-traveling and not world-traveling. Instead, in her understanding, "world traveling is a practice in which the multiplicitous self has access to an opening or aperture to different worlds," but the self remains "mine" and it is this mineness that gathers the world-traveling self together.[12]

In other words, as I understand it, these other worlds open the self to new possibilities and understandings, but the self does not leave the other aspects of herself behind. Just as Ortega finds that the playful aspect of herself comes to the fore with her fam-

9 Ibid., 26.
10 Ibid., 71.
11 Ibid., 88.
12 Ibid., 88.

ily or with other Latina friends and colleagues, she does not leave her playfulness behind when she inhabits the more traditional and all-too-serious realm of philosophy. It simply moves into the background and is generally not engaged. This is a region of her existence that comes to the fore in one world, and recedes in another, which is why she exists in-between.

This understanding of existence comes from Ortega's engagement with Heidegger. Understanding the self in terms of how it is, and how it becomes, in other words, as a temporal self, is key to Ortega's multiplicitous self. For Heidegger, the ecstasis of temporality means the self exists each moment not as a series of now moments, but rather as the past informing the present in anticipation of the future which includes our finitude. Ontological pluralism would suggest we leave the past, or other worlds behind as we world-travel. The multiplicitous self brings them with her.

There are concrete advantages to understanding the possibility for resistance with Ortega's multiplicitous self. Whereas for Lugones, resistance comes out of the "play of multiple visions" that allow the self to resist a "logic of purity," ultimately this multiple self, though nonfragmented, also lives multiple realities.[13] In Ortega's account, however, the "multiplicitous self can share specific spatial regions with others and also be in various worlds." Ortega's account thus provides multiple perspectives rather than "multiple crisscrossing realities." She does not "consider worlds as atomistic and thus not intersecting or crisscrossing."[14] Rather than being different persons in different worlds with no underlying 'I', Ortega's "Being-in-worlds is meant to capture the phenomenological way in which the multiplicitous self *is* or fares in various overlapping worlds, and thus it has an important existential component."[15]

Drawing on these multiple perspectives while remaining one self means that Ortega's multiplicitous self with its existential rather than ontological pluralism has the possibility of being an expert phenomenologist. As Ortega points out, "by being between

13 Ibid., 90, 93.

14 Ibid., 93.

15 Ibid., 93.

worlds and traveling worlds, the multiplicitous self can have access to alternative visions of self that are suppressed or erased in oppressive worlds." Situated at the limen, the multiplicitous self has more opportunities for "seeing differently and thus finding alternative visions of oneself and of worlds."[16]

If feminist phenomenology is about bringing the everyday to appearance so that we can better figure out where we want to go, what change needs to happen, then the multiplicitous self, the world-traveller, has the potential to be such a phenomenological expert because this self is never completely at home, can never be complacent, and so can't take anything for granted. Whereas for phenomenologists such as Heidegger, Merleau-Ponty, and Sartre, the pre-reflective self is inherently phenomenological, we go about our daily existence without consciously thinking about the ways things are, the multiplicitous self is not able to be at ease. For the multiplicitous self, the world rarely falls into the background; this self diverges from that of Heidegger for whom a "practical orientation… is the primary way in which the self is in the world."[17] The phenomenological method is meant to bring this everyday practical world that operates in the background into appearance. But the multiplicitous self is one step ahead. The multiplicitous self has the possibility of tending towards a critical conscious awareness of the ways in which we are in the world, since for this self the world is rarely ready-to-hand. Nothing has to be the way it is because the multiplicitous self has experienced other ways of being. And because this self is temporal, it can critically draw on past experiences to understand what is happening in this world at this moment, as well as to understand what it can be or emphasize different regions of existence in different worlds, all while remaining one multiplicitous self. It is, after all, often the juxtaposition in experiences that shows up the precariousness of the world and points towards alternative ways of being. For example, the way of being that is home is experienced more sharply through the homesickness that belongs to migrants and immigrants, and to those in

16 Ibid., 100.

17 Ibid., 60.

exile.

Nonetheless, as Ortega points out, living on the borders, that is, on the limen, is not itself "a sufficient condition for liberation."[18] For, if world-travelling becomes an every-day practice then it could be co-opted into the movement of publicness.[19] That is, even as the world-traveller sees "her differences or multiplicity," she may try "to preserve the status quo, all as part of an everyday attempt to survive within unwelcoming worlds."[20] Perhaps survival, Ortega suggests, includes having to give in, settle in, and accept "the norms, practices, and even the definitions of the multiplicitous self assigned by members of dominant groups." But, as she further contends, perhaps survival itself can also constitute an act of resistance.[21]

For Heidegger, the expert phenomenologist strives not to be at home. In his essay "Building Dwelling Thinking" he writes that mortals, that is, humans, are finite, temporal beings, and that the real "plight of dwelling" is not the homelessness that follows war and displacement, but rather that we "*must ever learn to dwell.*"[22] It is in fact Heidegger's preoccupation with the ontological, with relational ways of being over the ontic that could allow for such a claim. But Ortega's argument is that the ontic, the everydayness of oppressive material conditions cannot so easily be dismissed. For those who are literally homeless, Heidegger's claim is not helpful. Moreover, the experience of homelessness can lead to alternative insights into being. Accordingly, in balancing together both the ontological and the particularities of ontic material existence, Ortega opens new possibilities for theorizing oppression.

For example, let us consider Ortega's hometactics as employed by the multiplicitous self committed to resisting oppression, who is never at home, who is continually world-travelling and for

18 Ibid., 34.

19 See Martin Heidegger, "The They," in *Being and Time*, trans. Joan Stambaugh (Albany, N.Y.: SUNY Press, 1996), 107-122.

20 Ortega, *In-Between*, 127.

21 Ibid., 127.

22 Heidegger, "Building Dwelling Thinking," in *Poetry, Language, Thought*, trans. Alfred Hofstadter (New York: Harper Collins, 2001), 159.

whom "the question of home becomes a question of homes."[23] Hometactics are "temporal interventions aimed at producing variable situations but necessarily at abolishing a system of power."[24] It is a praxis that aims at "the production of a sense of familiarity in the midst of an environment or world in which one cannot fully belong due to one's multiple positions and instances of [what she calls] thin and thick not being at ease."[25] The multiplicitous self thus experiences at the same time both a "feeling of wanting to come home and that question of whether there is a home (or even homes) for [her]."[26]

This questioning belongs to being a phenomenal self who is never fully at home in the world because to be so would be to stop asking about what it means to dwell. For Heidegger, this questioning is tied to questioning the meaning of being—to not accepting a metaphysics of presence but to understanding that meaning is not given, but as dwelling, is rather relational, and existential. For Ortega, this questioning is a critical questioning, an asking about how we can live differently, resisting oppression and marginalization, and resisting the forces that engage us in oppressing others. In fact, as she points out, hometactics is a "taking advantage of opportunities as they present themselves." It is "an uncovering of what multiplicitous selves are already practicing in their everydayness, a disclosure of that which is already happening in [their] lived experience."[27]

Ortega's hometactics is thus thoroughly existential drawing on the spatiality of home as situation and the temporality of lived existence. It involves accepting the ambiguity inherent to both searching for a "sense of belonging while being aware that such belonging is not possible."[28] As such it is an amplification of Heidegger's claim that humans are the beings who question their own being.

---

23 Ortega, *In-Between*, 196.
24 Ibid., 202.
25 Ibid., 203.
26 Ibid., 196.
27 Ibid., 202-3.
28 Ibid., 207.

From the perspective of the multiplicitous self, Ortega revisits discussions of feminist standpoint theory and ultimately identity politics with the goal of defending their significance for feminism. Early manifestations of standpoint theory were critiqued for presuming an essential self who was granted a privileged critical position based on her relatedness to oppression and the insight that provided. Rather than beginning with an essential and authentic self understood in the sense of being atemporal and not open to the world, which would derail the project from the start, Ortega introduces the multiplicitous self into the discussion. It is this self's relational situatedness in multiple world in which she is never at ease that allows for, but does not guarantee, a critical perspective. Although Ortega explicitly rejects any articulation of an "authentic" self which would imply an inherent essence and not allow for the self's relational becoming, the self is nonetheless also real and shaped by her material conditions. Moreover, though she also explicitly rejects Heidegger's authentic self that relies on shared and inherited values, norms and practices, since the multiplicitous self has so many inherited pasts to draw on it could never be clear which one that would be, as we saw with Anzaldúa, the risk is paralysis. There is nonetheless a sense of shaping oneself through the choices one makes, a shaping developed through the practice of hometactics.

Accordingly, in her discussion of identity politics, Ortega shows how working with an understanding of the multiplicitous self means we do not have to choose between identity or coalitional politics. Nor do we have to choose between an identity politics understood as grounded in an objective reality, which implies an essential self, or alternatively in a subjective one dependent on the identities with which we identify. For Ortega, identities are both subjective and objective. An experience of oppression can be shared by those who are racialized, not because they are objectively the same, but because their racialized marking subjects them to similar experiences of oppression. As Ortega further points out, it cannot be overlooked that it is women of colour who have continued to support identity politics, and white feminists who have 'moved on'. Though subjectively, we can choose our alliances, we can choose with whom we identify, which can mean crossing over objective identity markers, nonetheless, racialization has objective ontic consequences that shape experiences of identity. Sensibly, Ortega points out that establishing identity politics in terms of an 'either/or' binary or even in terms of strategic essentialism, misses the point. As existential selves we are tied to a material world that we understand subjectively according to the ways we are relationally in the world and in-between worlds.

In other words, as Ortega claims, the "notions of identity and identity politics continue to be relevant even for a multiplicitous self that is in process and that occupies multiple social locations." The challenge she sets is to think about identity not in terms of "sameness, essence, or ahistoricity," but to develop an identity politics that does not support homogenization or lead to fragmentation.[29] Against essentialism, the *mestiza* consciousness, or that of the multiple self, has aspects that are often contradictory (for example bringing Heidegger and Latina philosophy together). Nonetheless, for Ortega, these contradictions can and do coexist in one self just as for Merleau-Ponty the phenomenal body allows for the incompossibles in a way that logic does not. My body gathers together "a nexus of living meanings" of incompossibles that emerge for example from seeing, touching, and hearing that cannot be collapsed into one another yet nonetheless belong to one body and open onto one world. Ortega takes Merleau-Ponty's insight a step further because the body of the multiplicitous self opens onto multiple worlds and in between-worlds. This body brings its incompossible habits and ways of being with it in world-travelling, but these ways do not remain in the background, they come to the fore as different worlds call for different habits of being. These habits of being—does one eat cake with a spoon or a fork?—are not trivial. They allow us to be at home or not at home, or somewhat at home in the world or worlds.

Similarly, if we take Heidegger's understanding of *Mitsein*, or being together, then we are always already in the world with

29 Ibid., 146.

others. In other words, for Heidegger, we are not locked in our solitude, which we must in some empathetic way bridge in order to be with others. Rather, even though as *Mitsein* we are often in a deficient mode of being with others, nonetheless, being with others is primordial to human existence. Accordingly, our identities as not given, as always becoming, are open to being shaped by our relations with others and with the world and worlds. Of course, Heidegger did not seem to understand the implications of his own thinking. His understanding of the self's relations with others, with the "they" or the public world ultimately involves a leveling down, a giving over to a kind of generality that is not one's own. Ortega, with other feminists, goes beyond the generalities of *das Man*. Being with others opens us both to oppression and to joy.

Ortega thus draws on Heidegger's existential phenomenology because it provides a helpful account of an epistemic subject that is temporal and not unified. At the same time this phenomenal subject is a being-in-one-world and thus "relentlessly Eurocentric."[30] A phenomenal subject who is in the world, or even who inhabits the world is insufficient for thinking beyond a Eurocentric paradigm. Accordingly, opening up the phenomenal subject to the multiplicitous self and to being between worlds provides a more compelling account for the critical perspective of feminist phenomenology that is tied to opposing oppression and marginalization, and to a phenomenology that has any critical potential for decolonization. In fact, from my perspective there is no going back for feminist phenomenology. Mariana Ortega's concept of the multiplicitous self who exists in-between worlds will become fundamental to any feminist or critical phenomenology that claims to oppose oppression and to provide rich descriptions of lived existence.

30 Ibid., 115.

CAN PHILOSOPHY LOVE?: REFLECTIONS AND ENCOUNTERS

Edited by Cindy Zeiher and Todd McGowen. London: Rowman and Littlefield, 2017

ALI ALIZADEH

One may feel initially sceptical about a book that purports to combine philosophy with love. And justifiably so. Have we not had enough of books that subject philosophy to the logic of feel-good, self-help, motivational publishing rackets? Will this volume not be yet another insincere, mediocre attempt at popularising philosophy *à la* Alain de Botton's bland bestsellers *Essays in Love*, *The Course of Love*, etc.? And is the coupling of philosophy with love—yes, the pun is intended—not, at best, a matter for acerbic satire and scandalous pornography, as graphically shown in the Marquis de Sade's notorious *La philosophie dans le boudoir*?

Thankfully, there's a lot more to the rapport between love and philosophy than the agendas of contemporary commercial publishers or the perversions of libertine satirists. For one thing, *love* is already imbedded in *philosophy*, as the Greek *philosophia* (φιλοσοφία) means, of course, the love (*philia*, φιλία) of wisdom (*sophia*, σοφία). Furthermore, it is not only anodyne celebrity writers but also rather serious contemporary philosophers who find love a worthy topic for intellectual enquiry. Alain Badiou's anointment of love as one of his grand, *evental* conditions of truth—on par with politics, science and art—and his *Éloge de l'amour* are two recent examples of philosophers' ongoing engagement with the questions of amorous attraction, attachment, and their consequences for thought and human subject. Finally, let us not forget that at least one kind of love—of the more mental, non-physical kind—that is, platonic love, is named after a philosopher.

But these observations do not sidestep the challenges of bringing love and philosophy together. Could this combination not result in a misrepresentation of love—which, even in its most platonic manifestation, has something to do with urges, desires and all that is uncontrollable and perhaps even irrational—due to the austere, cerebral dictates of philosophy? And, conversely, would the fusion of thinking and feeling not run the risk of subordinating contemplation to passion, the brain to the heart? Perhaps. But it seems to me that these objectionable syntheses would occur only if we think of philosophy as simply a (verbose) style of logical argumentation, and of love as some kind of quaint, incomprehensible mystery. To render love thinkable, then, one must also show that philosophy can be lovable. Such is the intention of Cindy Zeiher and Todd McGowan, the editors of *Can Philosophy Love?*

This collection has, generally speaking, two major strands, each originating in one aspect of the central contradiction of love's rapport with philosophy. These strands are—again, very broadly—idealism and psychoanalysis. The book brings together an impressive array of mostly younger philosophers, some of whom are already emerging as important figures in contemporary Continental thought. As such, whilst the general orientations of the perspectives in the book are the notoriously 'Continental'—*difficult* and *non-analytic*—figures of Hegel and Lacan, the authors are not given to the excessive linguistic convolutions of some Continental thinkers. There is, however, at the same time, a good deal of originality and flair in many of the pieces, which helps with obviating the perception that a philosophical enquiry may automatically turn the experience of love into an emotionless, over-intellectual discourse.

I'll address the book's Hegelian trajectory first, as it precedes the psychoanalytic provenance, at least chronologically. In the book's first chapter—following on from the editors' introduction in which they admit that "one of the great appeals of love is its resistance to our critical faculties"[1]—one of the book's editors, Todd McGowan, argues that love is not only one philosophical object amongst many, but that is it the exemplary philosophical object—and perhaps even *the* philosophical objective—*par excellence*; and that it is via a thinker often credited with such a proposal, the great Georg Wilhelm Friedrich Hegel, that it may be shown that not only is philosophy compatible with love, but that philosophy may even depend on (a theory of) love for its sustenance. McGowan suggests that love is "the animating principle of the system" of Hegel's early thought[2], and, even after "the concept (*Begriff*) has taken over the central place in Hegel's system",[3] love remains a model for key elements of his later philosophy, such as the concept itself.[4]

But what, precisely, is love according to Hegel and the tradition of thought which follows on from him? McGowan writes:

> Love for Hegel has nothing to do with narcissistic self-affirmation through the other. It is rather a profound disturbance for the subject's identity. Hegel's definition of love has a radicality that he would sustain in his love-inspired definition of the concept. He writes, 'love can only occur against the same, against the mirror, against the echo of our essence'.[5]

It is important to note that this definition of love does not have purely or even primarily ethical implications—insofar as it might be seen as an injunction to love the truly differentiated other and to not love the false other (one's own fantasy) of the same, as reflected in a mirror—and that its primary topic is the subject. The *profound disturbance* that McGowan notes is not merely some kind of personal, aesthetic or emotional intensity—as may be found in a Hollywood fantasy such as *Eat, Pray, Love*—but a *radicality* that breaks our perception of who we are, and makes the subject (as

1 Cindy Zeiher and Todd McGowan, eds. *Can Philosophy Love?: Reflections and Encounters* (London: Rowman and Littlefield, 2017), xii.
2 Ibid., 4.
3 Ibid.
4 Ibid., 6.
5 Ibid., 11.

opposed to the fantastic image of the subject, i.e. identity) possible and thinkable. Following on from this, it may be said that it is love (and perhaps *only* love?) that makes it possible for one to repudiate the narcissistic falsehood of hearing only an echo of one's own essence, and to approach a true subjectivity that entails the capacity for thinking the concept. Love, then, is the crucial prerequisite for philosophy.

As we shall see, Lacan and the Lacanians have things to say about this idealistic account of love. For now, I'd like to note that one of the great virtues of *Can Philosophy Love?* is the editors' inclusion of essays that challenge their own theses. Frank Ruda's "Love-Life" and Agon Hamza's "Against Love as a Political Category" take issue, in different ways, with the central philosophic prominence accorded to love by McGowan. Ruda agrees with McGowan's account in so far as he too notes that, apropos of (the young) Hegel, "love is the concept";[6] but this love-as-concept must avoid "the mortification of love" found in other intellectual or transcendent abstractions of love's immanence (e.g. in the Kantian *cosmopolitan love*).[7] To do so, Hegel must claim that, whilst love is infinite or transcendent, it also, at the same time, possesses a sensual and living "form in which this infinity manifests"; and, therefore, the eventual destination of amorous subjectivity is not the province of thinking and the philosophical, but "that of feeling".[8]

Hamza takes issue with the political implications of the idealization of love. Citing a love letter from Hegel's most famous, most heretical disciple, Karl Marx, in which Marx distinguishes the radically transformative love that he feels for the letter's addressee (his wife, Jenny von Westphalen) from a more speculative, more ideal kind of love (e.g. a politicized sentiment such as "love for the proletariat as a class"[9]), Hamza argues that the dialectical tension here is not so much between the particularity of romantic love (for a sensual other) and the universality of fraternal love (for

6 Ibid., 109.
7 Ibid.
8 Ibid., 110.
9 Ibid., 135.

one's comrades), but the constitutive, absolute separation between the fields of love and politics.[10] Furthermore, Hamza insists—in a fundamentally dialectical, Maoist or Badiouian spirit—that the two should be kept separated, and that it is perfectly possible, even desirable, for one to achieve true (political) subjectivity without recourse to any kind of love. Hamza reminds us that even Hegel himself, when considering history, "would differentiate the concept of politics that is produced by political history, from the concept of love at stake in the history of love;"[11] and that, ultimately, if love has a political task, it is nothing other than to "fight for preserving *intimacy*" from domination by "political ideology."[12]

But what is intimacy, and do we really want it? And is love really possible or even desirable in the first instance? This scepticism is the basic premise for the psychoanalytic direction of the essays collected in this volume, and this trajectory is exemplified by the notoriously aporetic Jacques Lacan's assertion, "*il n'y a pas de rapport sexuel.*"[13] As shown in the book's final chapter by its other editor, Cindy Zeiher, whilst for Hegel and Hegelians love possesses or allows for the possession of something—the concept, feelings, intimacy, etc.—for Lacan love is founded on possessing nothing whatsoever, on "how we experience lack."[14] As Zeiher writes:

> Lacan indicates that the function of love is an endeavour to make up for the lack of sexual relationship—that is, the paradox that although loving another subject constitutes a whole, demanding love in return is to ask for the loved one to reveal and confront his or her own lack. The specificity of love as the most logical signifier of alienation is crucial if love is to be recognized by the subject.[15]

As with Hegel's idealization of love, then, Lacan's non-idealization of love is also a complex, paradoxical matter. Zeiher shows,

---

10 Ibid., 136.
11 Ibid., 137.
12 Ibid., 144.
13 Perhaps Lacan's best known slogan: "There is no sexual relationship." Eds.
14 Ibid., 301.
15 Ibid.

via considering and reconciling Badiou's and Alenka Zupančič's somewhat divergent theories of love, that the (Lacanian) lack may itself be seen as a thing—in fact, as *the* Thing (*das Ding*)—because, precisely due to its lacking an "entirely visible, locatable or trusted" content, it posits a love that transcends mere reality and "promises access to the Real."[16] As Zeiher notes, Lacan famously claimed in *Seminar VIII* that "*love is giving what you don't have to someone who does not want it.*"[17] But this statement should not be read as a witty dismissal of love. It is an exact formulation of the absence of sexual or amorous rapport, and the fact that, according to this formulation, love is only made possible due to this absence. It is precisely because the beloved negates the lover's projection of his or her own negation that, far from the beloved becoming the repository of the lover's (narcissistic) fantasy of an other who is in fact simply a reflection of one's own (absent) self, the lover instead comes face to face with the radically transformative "core of subjective difference."[18]

There is more than a whiff of the Hegelian *negation of the negation* in this description of Lacan's theory of love. In many ways, the overall project of *Can Philosophy Love?* may be described as a fusion of Lacanian and Hegelian perspectives, a synthesis which is proving to be one of the most fertile and interesting currents in today's Continental philosophy. One may discern, for example, a semi-Hegelian philosophy of art in Jelica Šumič's explicitly Lacanian readings of medieval mystics in her contribution to the volume, "Towards a Limitless Love or Mystical 'Jouissance of Being.'" Šumič contends that the jouissance or the ecstatic quality of mystical texts (those written by female mystics, in particular) is the product of an encounter with an invisible, unsayable divinity, and that it "arises from the relationship that cannot be written, that is the sexual relationship."[19] Importantly, the impossibility of writing (directly and prosaically) about one's relationship with God, far from resulting in a Wittgensteinnian "injunction to silence", com-

16 Ibid., 305.
17 Ibid., 303.
18 Ibid.
19 Ibid., 48.

pels "the mystic to speak, succeeds to inscribe itself in writing."[20] This "fundamental contamination of the signifier by jouissance"[21] does not seem so different to Hegel's view of art (and of quasi-mystical Romantic poetry, in particular) as material works animated by the Spirit.

My reading of this collection, as focussed on the Hegelian and Lacanian themes and perspectives, does not necessarily exclude contributions that address the question of love's thinkability via philosophers other than Hegel and Lacan. These include Sigi Jöttkandt's fascinating "Cordelia's Kiss" which considers an episode in Kierkegaard's *Enten – Eller* (*Either/Or: A Fragment of Life*), a work which, according to Jöttkandt, "invites a reading as an allegory of Hegelian dialectics",[22] an allegory which comes undone as a result of what seems strikingly similar to a kind of linguistic jouissance in the work itself, in the signifier of "a sacred kiss."[23] Monique Rooney's "Love's Intermediary: The Aesthetics of Rousseau's *Amour de Soi*" also draws on literary compositions by a philosopher—Rousseau's *Narcisse* (*Narcissus: Or, the Lover of Himself*)and *Pygmalion*—to deconstruct the opposition between Rousseau's potentially idealistic *'amour de soi'*, and the less ideal, far less desirable *amour propre.*[24] In short, even the contributions that do not openly or substantially refer to Hegel or Lacan can be seen to be concerned with Hegel's crucial discovery of love as a philosophical category, and with Lacan's problematization of this discovery.

What, then, can be said about love's relationship with philosophy? Is this too a kind of Lacanian non-relation which, due to its impossibility, compels a philosopher to write about love even more obsessively? Or is there no thinking without thinking about love (or in love), as a young Hegel might have it? Whichever view

20 Ibid., 49.

21 Ibid.

22 Ibid., 193.

23 Ibid., 203.

24 In French both *amour de soi* and *amour propre* means something akin to 'self-love' in English; Rousseau uses them to distinguish love of one's self based something intrensic from self-love based on the esteem of others.' For Rousseau, the former is natural, the latter artificial. Eds.

one finds more compelling—and I think it would be fair to say that most of the thinkers included in this insightful collection take something from both approaches—one cannot deny that love is far from unthinkable. Love may be the subject of innumerable cultural products of our world, many of them superficial, exploitative and ideological, but this book is most certainly not one of those. It shows us that love is an area rich with profound and serious thinking and writing.

www.ingramcontent.com/pod-product-compliance
Lightning Source LLC
LaVergne TN
LVHW090942080826
845145LV00003B/861

* 9 7 8 0 7 7 1 4 3 1 2 6 5 *